PENGUIN BOOKS

FACTS AND FANCIES

Armando Iannucci was born in Glasgow in 1963 and studied English at Glasgow and Oxford universities. He started writing a thesis on Milton and seventeenth-century religious poetry, and this is his first public admission that it will never be completed. He was one of the creators of *On the Hour*, *The Day Today* and *Knowing Me, Knowing You ... with Alan Partridge*, and he presents his own comedy show, *The Friday Night Armistice*, on BBC2. He broadcasts regularly on BBC Radio One and Four, and writes a fortnightly column for the *Guardian*. He has one wife and a smaller version of himself, and they all live in the rough end of Buckinghamshire.

D1362653

FACTS AND FANCIES

Armando Iannucci

PENGUIN BOOKS

PENGUIN BOOKS

Published by the Penguin Group
Penguin Books Ltd, 27 Wrights Lane, London W8 5TZ, England
Penguin Putnam Inc., 375 Hudson Street, New York, New York 10014, USA
Penguin Books Australia Ltd, Ringwood, Victoria, Australia
Penguin Books Canada Ltd, 10 Alcorn Avenue, Toronto, Ontario, Canada M4V 3B2
Penguin Books (NZ) Ltd, 182–190 Wairau Road, Auckland 10, New Zealand

Penguin Books Ltd, Registered Offices: Harmondsworth, Middlesex, England

First published by Michael Joseph 1997
Published in Penguin Books 1997
1 3 5 7 9 10 8 6 4 2

Printed in England by Clays Ltd, St Ives plc

for Rachael, with all my love

ACKNOWLEDGEMENTS

Umpteen-and-one thanks must go to my editor Maggie Pringle for patiently coaxing this book out of me through three years of persuasion, and for not fretting at the printer's when the final pages hadn't been written. Thanks also to Roger Alton and all those nameless voices I've spoken to over the phone at the *Guardian*. A big thanks too to the funny Mr David Schneider for taking time out to read my stuff and then prepare what amounted to a thorough but invaluable report. Peter Baynham and Sarah Smith were also kind enough to give me the benefit of their splendid comedy brains. I have to confess to trying out ideas and half-formed thoughts on unwitting friends in the course of apparently casual conversations, so apologies to anyone who's surprised to discover the products of those moments here. Peter Bennett-Jones, Anna Wilks, Emma Cockshut and Loretta Sacco all helped get the book up and running and I'm grateful for their help and advice.

My biggest debt of gratitude is to my wife, Rachael, who not only came up with perfect suggestions as the book was being written, but literally shielded me from every domestic upheaval when I did my stupid impression of an angst-ridden author needing perfect quiet for his work. This she did by building me an out-house in the garden. It was great.

CONTENTS

MY INTRODUCTION TO THIS BOOK

Writing a book is an undertaking far more horrific than I'd ever imagined. Not only must the writer come up with several tens of thousands of words, not all of them the same, but he or she must arrange them in an order that makes some sort of sense to the first-time reader. It's no use starting your book 'Linford Christie stepped into the horse-box bemused by the wall of mushrooms which stood grinning at the back' if you have no intention of taking these ideas any further. To start a book with this sentence, but then take your eye off the ball for a moment and end up writing a twenty-thousand word guide to Polish war memorials, deserves the highest criticism. It's a fault that took me many months of practice to avoid.

Others have been less meticulous. I'm surely not the only one to have noticed that Will Hutton's otherwise admirably written economics bestseller *The State We're In* opens with the sentence 'This book has been carefully graded so that you can begin with one or two elementary dishes yet soon be able to set out a full Thai meal with all its unique flavours.' Nor is there any earthly explanation other than sheer authorial incompetence for a few stray lines in Stephen Hawking's *A Brief History of Time* which, at the end of a brilliant explanation of the symbiotic relationship between quantum theory and relativity, seductively hinting at a unified theory of gravity, suddenly continue:

Bevin let out a gasp of astonishment and playful pleasure at the Professor's remarks. 'Ooh boy,' she yelped, like a cat. 'Tell it to me one more time, 'cos

I'm on fire, particle man!' She remembered now their curiously interrupted lovemaking from the previous night and resolved to hammer the door shut this time.

The remaining ninety pages revert to a discussion of particle/wave duality within light emissions.

Consistency of subject is therefore a prerequisite for even the most vaguely competent stab at a book. But there are more basic concerns that have to be addressed first. For example, what size of book do you intend to write? To resolve the issue, I spent months locked in negotiations with my editor and various 3D cardboard models of my proposed work. One model was for a book five millimetres thick and four metres high. I'm told it was life-size. We dismissed the notion as impractical and in the end we came up with a prototype new size invented from scratch with some measuring tape and crêpe paper. I'd always been a fan of the thickness of *Nicholas Nickleby* and *Wild Swans* and wanted to aim for something similar. I was also impressed by the sensible height of the Inspector Morse series. After some arguments and tears, we agreed that the final book-mould should deposit into people's hands something thicker than J. G. Ballard but without bal- looning into Robert Ludlum.

After size, comes content. Again, this must be settled at the deepest level, including agreement on all the letters. As I soon discovered when I began this appalling project, an author and his copyright lawyer are obliged to negotiate the publishing rights of each letter of the alphabet individually. After about a year of expensive fights, we reached agree- ment on all the vowels and most consonants. However, 'n', 'm' and 'S' (but not 's') produced deadlock. These had all been bought up by Donna Summer for her comeback tour. So none of these letters will be appearing in this volume, I'm afraid. If you're disappointed, then I suggest you read a book about Thermonuclear Submarines, which I can guarantee will be full of the stuff. I'm also grateful to Marjory

Stafford, widow of the inventor of 'z', for permission to use her late husband's letter in my chapter on Byzantine pizzazz.

As for subject matter, I was initially interested in writing an encyclopaedia of folklore, and indeed the first draft of this book went pretty much along those lines. However, one or two changes have occurred along the way. My editor made improvements in the structure, first by eliminating the encyclopaedic element and then by producing a chart which showed how much the idea of a book about folklore is hated by all of the reading public. I'm extremely grateful for her gentle emendations.

About 43% of this book appeared as some of my regular Column Inches pieces in the *Guardian*, though I've slightly up-dated or retouched them for the purpose of being better. The rest is mostly new, with the exception of the short story **Us and Them**, which first appeared in the January '94 publication of Nabisco Biscuits' In-House Newsletter, *Crumbler*, and the title chapter **Facts and Fancies**, whose text is actually based on the computer print-out of the gene map of the tuberculosis virus.

None of the work you're about to read is meant to be funny. I am deeply serious about this. This is a literary work, not the gaggy spewings of some whore-clown. I do not perform comedic jigs for the misguided delight of a baying audience of readers. I am an artist, and all art is serious. Michelangelo's saints don't sit on whoopee cushions nor do Francis Bacon's Popes chuckle. I've gone through this book and erased all the jokes. If any are still here, then I can only conclude that my editor has taken another look at her blasted charts and secretly inserted some jokes of her own. Damn her to hell.

Since falling in with her and her book-possetting cronies, I've become party to a shameful trade practice which I now feel it my duty to snitch on here, namely that the endings to most volumes of non-fiction currently produced in this country are being fixed by overseas betting syndicates. If you think it beyond the imagination of good writers to sink into the mire, then just look at the following paragraph which ends John Pilger's most recent manuscript recounting his trip to East Timor:

The weapons industry still flourishes in this land of the impoverished, and the rain that nurtures it is a rain of hard cash poured out of Western aid budgets. It's as grim a certainty that the local arms factory will be in constant production this winter as that Dunfermline will have to pull out all the stops if they want to avoid bitter defeat against Hamilton on Saturday.

Insightful analogy? Maybe, but British non-fiction writers are big business in certain parts of the world, and in flea markets all over Thailand and Singapore illegal bets are being placed on the conclusion of their works. How else can you explain these lines I found near the end of Bernard Levin's latest scroll:

Solzhenitsyn then turned and left me alone in the room, and as I watched his frail yet curiously powerful form withdraw, I could only tremble at his parting words: that Russia is in a kind of waking death and that Berwick manager Tom Hendrie may face an upset when his youthful side meet Dumbarton at the weekend.

A brief glance at the Sunday sports pages at the time of publication will tell you that Alexander Solzhenitsyn was indeed no footballing novice. But why the intrusion of Scottish football speculation in an otherwise dull tome about the elderly? Under normal conditions, the odds on someone like Jonathan Meades ending his restaurant guides with a reference to Scottish Division Two must be enormous, so obviously somebody somewhere would have made a lot of money when last Spring this appeared:

All in all then, extraordinary walnuts, in a quince sauce dribbled on to the plate as exquisitely as veteran East Fife striker Steve Archibald dribbled a late equalizer past Clyde on Saturday. Lunch £90.

Either pre-written concluding paragraphs to pieces are being intercepted and doctored by nefarious Eastern gamblers or – and it makes me wretch rather loudly even to write this – our authors are accepting cash payments to end their works in an agreed manner.

And so, bobbing on this vat of deceit, uncorrupted sails my book, immune to the taints of Scottish soccer. It is the purest entity. I have no great hopes for it. It will not change the world, and will only subtly affect the way we live now. If it succeeds in promoting peace and understanding among even one fifteenth of the world's population then it will have more than paid for its production costs. If it deters crime, and destroys at a stroke the international drugs problem, then this will be a reward significantly greater than any cash advance.

Books are like children; they get nursed, spill soup, then leave to start a family. Your individual responses to this book are that very family, and the money you hand over is my grandchild. My only hope is that you're not currently reading this volume in the £1 section of a second-hand bookshop in Leeds in 1998. If you are, then I don't want to know for I would rather the financial disappointment of this treacherous literary project remain as secret as Stranraer's chances are forlorn of avoiding relegation at the end of the season.

Cuba, January 1997

NOISE

Imagine noise was solid.

At 6 pm, outside Hebdon Bridge's Shopper's Paradise, great puddles of music lie around on the pavement, swept out of the arcade at close of business. Unplayed saxophone melodies, still wrapped in Tannoy, are bundled neatly for collection.

At night, families deposit arguments outside their back-door, bin-bagged and double-wrapped, for fear of neighbourly recognition.

The noise slick from the factory devastates the local landscape. Clanks and thuds clog up the stream and deafen the salmon while a great billowing cloud of hum settles on wheatfields, producing noisy beer four months later.

After the failed coup, over one hundred and fifty collaborators are lined up against the walls of the State Prison, and shrieked at. Their widows are called in the next morning and left to collect the bodies. Some of their husbands have been called names.

Tests on the Tutting Bomb near completion. Once dropped, the bomp disperses a disapproving tut across a five-mile radius. Buildings are left intact, but the populace is wracked by guilt in seconds.

A young woman hurriedly places her crying into a plastic bag and hides it in a jewellery box as she hears her husband come through the front door.

I think about noise a lot, and wonder whether our ears are getting too full. Today, noise is *the* defining sensation of our inter-active experiences. A cashpoint machine without its sober 'blup', a computer game that did not 'shhzz' each time you severed the head off Medrath, the Rampaging Girl of Alaska, a supermarket checkout desk that couldn't 'pmmn' at every jar of Nutella that passed under it, would all seem pointless and unconvincing. Noise supplies potency: the 'wuuoowuuoowuuoo' of the car alarm on a Peugeot is the modern-day roar of the tiger.

Maybe one day we'll seek to enhance the natural world's offerings with artificially produced sounds of our own, so that animals will be supplied with added studio-enhanced rustles, or multi-tracked growls. Species may be bred with better quality 'realistic' sounds and placed back in their natural habitat. Using these fresh digitally re-mastered calls of the wild, the creatures would not only fare better, due to more effective snarling, but give greater listening pleasure to their colleagues.

I think a lot about the quality of sounds we're going to produce in the future, and how they compare to all the sounds we made in the past. To make the comparison, I've steeped myself in all the literature on the subject, especially histories of noise:

How did noise begin?

First came the Big Bang, a single, infinitesimally short concentration of uproar containing the essence of every subsequent sound. In one voluminous note was amassed all the future possibilities of noise: the creaking of a stair, the rustle of a falling leaf against the side of an amputee, the howl of a zebra. Every sound we have, and every sound that will be, was present at this primal clamour, which instantly parped its load across the universe, scattering sounds over a thousand galaxies so that today traces of disparate and faint noises can still be detected at the furthest edges of space. The sound of a glove puppet being torn by wolves circulates Jupiter, while beyond Saturn lies the noise of a small onion hitting formica and the crack of an elephant tusk on the bonnet of a Talbot Horizon. Most recently, microphones have detected a cloud of over thirteen hundred variations of Lulu's whine beyond Neptune.

The Bang poured noise even into the most isolated folds of our physics. In parallel universes, worlds exist similar to our own in every way except that carpets can whistle, or that nuclear alert sirens in emergencies blast across each city the sound of water filling a metal pan. One such Earth has silent night clubs. Throngs of young people attend these dingy underground caverns, located in the least beautiful parts of the city, ready to dance to the latest bits of quiet pumped out a speaker-system bigger than a carnival. The music is mostly long pauses, but occasionally aggrieved silences are played between midnight and two. Other hiati enjoyed by the clubbers are the uniform lull on Thursdays and the sudden hush on Ladies' Nights.

[*The Cambridge History of Noise*, Volume One: Whooping Before Christ, CUP pp 3–4]

Have you ever tried sitting in silence? The injunction our parents gave us when we were toddlers screaming for chocolate mice while banging a china cup off our mum's lips is as hard to follow now as it ever was. At home or at work, we seek the companionship of noise to help alleviate the sheer ordinariness of our activity. Music pumps life back into the suffocating asthmatic attacks of silence, and if music is unavailable we quickly attempt an emergency substitute, tapping away on the edge of the desk like woodpeckers on heroin or transforming deck-shoes into orchestras. Anything to impose rhythm on an otherwise badly regulated day.

And now we have the added advantage of being able to carry our selected noises with us. The slim, high-precision technology of the Walkman makes it easier, and more acceptable, to pump music into our heads while we're on the bus, making love, or sitting in on jury service. The effect is totally transformative. The Walkman has enabled us to turn our music collection into a sort of soundtrack to play over the continuous film of our lives. 'Music From The Movies' can turn a humdrum jog around the forgotten turds of the city park into an heroic escape from an enemy ammunition dump. Our headphones transform an approaching pushchair into a dying planet, and a kid's mother into the Crab Nebula.

And yet what we're doing is turning a highly sophisticated art-form into a designer tinnitus for modern-day living. Anyone who insists on going shopping without wanting to hear a background orchestral arrangement of 'Uptown Girl' while trying on shoes is treated to a mixture of curiosity and pity, like someone whose brother has just died. Music takes us from the bed to the butcher's. We can cross the Atlantic to Guns'n'Roses. Mongrels can relax to high-frequency Eurythmics piped into kennels, while Lena Martell is common in most hospices.

Manchester is now experimenting with the quick relaying of on-site background music to accident victims. A fleet of cars with loudspeakers is on stand-by, ready to respond to any emergency call-out. Upon arrival at the crash scene they will act as a back-up service to the more direct efforts of the police and ambulance units, by piping the comforting sounds of Enya and Vangelis around the victim. These cars are equipped with a siren in A Minor.

Meanwhile, where is silence, and what does it sound like?

Experimenters recorded silence on the world's finest tape, and then turned the volume up. They heard a hiss. This proved not to be the magnified sound of a background atmosphere or even the enhanced resonances of the tape machine itself. Instead, it was proved conclusively that the hiss was the sound of a hundred million tiny men screaming because they couldn't be heard. Tests with powerful electron microscopes confirmed the discovery.

[*Journal of Audiological Culture*, Volume 8: Rasping and the Decline of the Modern Spirit, p 45]

Today, silence is sinful. It's located only in those tiny moments between momentous events, such as a sudden cardiac arrest and the subsequent howling of a granddaughter, or between high spirits on a speedboat and the moment when they result in a manslaughter; tiny spots of inactivity pregnant with disturbing consequence. We don't like silences much these days. You tend to know where you are with noise.

Silence is when sound has a think. Silence sits in the chair of a kidnapped uncle. It is the correct answer to an unasked question. Silence is a sucked shout, an ear on cold turkey, numb noise, two arguments cancelling each other out, a failed hurricane, the bellowing of a dead man. Silence is the sound of a pig that has been rashered.

[*Cambridge History of Noise*, Volume 2: Clanging In the Age of Enlightenment, p 108]

Somehow, a thing isn't right until it can make a sound. Maybe this comes from birth, when any child who emerges taciturn from the womb is slapped about a bit until it responds, like a broken telly being made to work again. As we grow up, we're enticed by voluble foodstuffs that snap, crackle, pop, crunch, smack, bubble and squeak their way down the infant gullet. Our adolescence is dominated by pop, rhythm and snogging (a thoroughly onomatopoeic word when you think about the sound four wet lips make when twisted ninety degrees out of alignment to their respective mouths), and our heroes today are bass guitarists rather than Douglas Bader.

Since the Second World War, collective memory has become defined almost exclusively by music, as nostalgia is prompted more and more by recollections of the sounds of the Fifties and its subsequent decades. Hair, fashion, and the type of person you're meant to get into a fight with on a beach are all being defined by the style of music that's listened to at the time, so that records and now CDs start dissolving into the past the moment they're released, like little mouthfuls of sherbet. Singles acquire significance not through how they sound but through how we remember they sounded as we heard them for the first time, while washing a car, growing up in Bolton, committing an offence, or walking past a crêperie.

One of the Nineteen Nineties' more interesting sociological twitches has been the development of classical music as a mode of background therapy. The efforts of Russian orchestras and monks with recording contracts are being marketed as stress capsules, tools for mental relief which the listener can wallow in at home like some catalogue-purchased sauna at the bottom of the garden. Today, music is packaged and labelled like bits of cow, chopped up and prepared for any one of the buyer's dietary preferences. We can select tapes of orchestral music to drive to, volumes of Classic Romance to have on stand-by for last-minute seductions, Classics to Cook To, Classic Divorce Tracks, One Hundred Orchestral Masterpieces To Become Bankrupt To, Classics for Petting, and Classics to Read Non-Fiction By.

I, for example, am writing this to Mussorgsky's 'Songs and Dances of Death'. I don't know what they're about, since they're in Russian, but I imagine death comes into it quite a lot. It sounds like it does. I imagine Mussorgsky sweated his musical guts out getting these pieces right; tackling death head on can be back-breaking work, even if it's just to come up with a song and a dance, so at the end of it, the exhausted Romantic probably felt like packing up his metronome and going for a dunk in a spa. Yet to me, they're just pleasant sounds coming from the radio, a sort of aural ruled paper to help me write.

Why do we respond so rudely to carefully crafted noise? If The Scottish Ballet Company turned up to dance round our office would we be so unappreciative? Would we use a David Hockney original as a place mat for a casserole, or Richard Roger's Lloyds Building as just somewhere we can dump our coats? Are there not other senses I need to keep occupied before I can settle to work? Maybe spend some moments at the start of the day releasing a few background smells – olive and caramel potpourri, broccoli-scented joss-sticks, bottled hedge – or arrange some subtle and pleasant textures across my chair and desk – bat's fur and gooseberry skin lampshades – to caress as I labour?

Maybe it's just because, like the five billion other human beings on this planet, I'm just scared of being on my own. Background music cancels our sense of isolation from other people but, unlike recorded speech, doesn't remind us what a bother it is trying to get on with them. It's a happy compromise, and one which more and more of us may be content to sit through for the rest of our lives.

On January 22nd, 1987, fifty-two-year-old electrician Peter Manion volunteered to have the world's first permanent music implant. A selection of music was edited into a continuous loop lasting three hours and fifty-four minutes, and then digitally relayed onto a small chip the size of a pea. The music chip was then surgically inserted into the brain, to one side of the frontal lobe, while the sensation of quadrophonic reproduction was affected by four smaller speakers placed within the left and right frontal and rear cortexes.

Much debate had gone into the final selection of music that was to play endlessly in the patient's brain. The original plan was for a specially convened committee of musicologists, surgeons and lay concert-goers to draw up a definitive list of pieces to be included on the tape loop. A special composition, 'Serenade For Peter's Head', by the composer Sonia Levinson had also been commissioned by the selection committee to be included on the tape.

The piece was to be premiered on the eve of the historic operation at London's Purcell Rooms in front of Princess Alexandra. However, that day Mr Manion and his family succeeded in the Court of Appeal in gaining the right to have sole control over the selection of music for the implant.

At exactly 9 am the next day, after final clearance had been given by the courts, the operation proceeded, and a small capsule containing the following pieces of music was inserted into the patient's head: 'An Evening With Cleo Laine and Johnny Dankworth', 'The 1986 Edinburgh Military Tattoo', Barbara Streisand's 'The Way We Were', 'Trisch Trasch Polka' by Johann Strauss, 'Classic Commercial Cuts, Volume Two, featuring the Music from the Northern Waterways Advert', 'Vienna' by Ultravox (at the request of Mr Manion's thirty-year-old daughter) and James Galway's 'Flutes of the Forest'.

The operation was a qualified success. An imperfection in the chip resulted in the music being played at seven-eighths its original speed, with a resultant lowering of pitch. However, Peter Manion expressed himself delighted with the result, and further surgery was deemed unnecessary. The first man to have a continuous personal source of background music went on to live a normal and happy life. Blood pressure, heart rate and stress levels all measured lower than average, and the patient later professed to having attained a certain sense of calm and even serenity in his life. The selection of music was released on CD, and sales over the next four years eclipsed those of all others on the market. Many people were noticeably transformed by the music, and requests for the implant operation increased a thousandfold: the requests were very specific though, asking for exactly the same selection of music, and at seven-eighths speed.

Tests by neurological anthropologists into this behaviour are not yet concluded, but initial findings seem to indicate that the Manion Tape Loop has, perhaps by sheer coincidence, assembled a sequence of sounds which most perfectly attains total resonance with the natural rhythms of the emotional and spiritual cycles of man. If these findings are confirmed by later tests, then it may be that we are on the threshold of a significant transformation in human behaviour. A continuous and comprehensive transmission of the loop throughout the inhabited world may result in the diminution and even extinction of aggressive behaviour in man, and the liberalization of a benign and uniform human pleasantness. The Twenty-First Century may be radically different from the one we know now, in which total happiness may be swiftly established with a tape compilation of James Galway, Cleo Laine and The Edinburgh Tattoo, and at the acceptable expense of silence.

[*New Harmony Scientific Quarterly*, Volume xxiii, pp 304–309: The Manion Tape Loop: Benign Effects of MOR Immersion.]

CULT CANCELLED

How do you start a religious cult? Beginners' kits are hard to come by, so presumably it's all down to personal charisma and a good speaking voice. Yet, most cult leaders are wan hairy men who look like lecturers in Land Economics at the University of Strathclyde; hardly the sort of bloke you'd imagine your daughter literally going nuts for. But somehow they manage to succeed in copping off with people's daughters by the commune-full.

So how do they start? Say a forty-three-year-old man called Philip Dawsons wanted to start a cult, what does he do once he's perfected a weird stare and not shaved for a month? He could develop a philosophy for living which was as original as it was dependent on young women having sexual intercourse with him for the propagation of more true believers, but this relies on getting someone else to accept both the philosophy and the sex bit. Without these key moments of revelation, what Philip Dawsons would have is a cult of one.

It may be that all around the world mysterious or dangerous cults of one have quietly established themselves in people's houses. For example, Sandra McKinnon, a militant Judao-Hindu sect devoted to the overthrow of paternalistic family structures in France, whose headquarters is Sandra McKinnon's house, 103 Caghill Road, Leeds. There's the Domish People of Antwerp, based at 28 Riverside Gardens, Cardiff. Or the Branch-Wilhemina Church of Christ Patterson, contacted care of Steven Patterson, PO Box 91, County Antrim.

But a cult can't have respectable status unless it recruits at least enough people to fill a discreet conference centre and – given cult leaders tend to adopt a ridiculous system of theosophy, more likely than not based on the premise that coughing is the secret language of angels, and the Fourth Horseman of the Apocalypse is Bronchitis – recruitment isn't that simple.

~~Some cults get round this by watering down their system of belief so~~ that it becomes more easy to accept. For example, there's the Car Boot Cult, which started off as a counter-revolutionary group of quasi-Nazis based in Austria (*Der Karbütts*) but which over the years has softened its line to the present-day advocacy of a system of boot sales as a means of picking up bargains on a Saturday afternoon. Among the millions who are members of the Car Boot Cult are still many militants, who believe that Hitler could have more easily achieved his master-dream by organizing car-boot sales across all of Western Europe.

Only last year, plans were discovered proposing the organization of a giant boot sale for a hundred thousand blond men on the site of the original Nuremberg Rallies, while foundations for the construction of a massive and powerful car-boot about two hundred metres long have only recently been uncovered beneath a Geneva sports stadium. One should therefore never forget the origins of this seemingly harmless movement. The next time you buy a used strimmer from someone called Jonathan Courtney at a car-boot sale in Cuddicot, look deep into his eyes, because he's probably a Nazi.

Many people are put off joining cults by the notorious suicide clause at the end of most entry forms. All cults require its members to kill themselves periodically in a display of loyalty, usually while representatives of the state government are arriving at the group's headquarters with water-cannon. Some cults are even stricter: forty-seven members of the Silent Badger, a Methodist anti-democracy militia based in Derby, disembowelled themselves when the North West Water Authority returned a cheque they'd forgotten to sign.

Ritual Suicide is one of the most popular events at the biannual

Cult Olympics, held this year at a secret gun camp in Arizona. Here, cults from all around the world let their hair down and take part in a number of nihilo-competitive events such as Synchronized Self-Immolation, and the Men's Four by One Hundred Days Hunger Strike. Plans for this year's Olympics include a spectacular closing ceremony in which a carefully co-ordinated poison gas attack on Stockholm will kill selected people in a crowded shopping centre to spell from above the words 'See You In Sweden, '99!'

Let's return then to our hopeful cultist, Mr Philip Dawsons. Through advertising in a number of personal columns he's managed to recruit five young women to his organization. He did this by meeting each one of them for a series of candle-lit dinners at the Thai King Restaurant, Southwold and delighting them with his witty conversation. The problem is, though, that none of them are aware they've joined a cult, thinking instead that they've each just started going out with a pleasant if slightly dull forty-three-year-old who likes Thai food and the Bible. Philip has yet to introduce them to each other, but at least he has the beginnings of a good sect. He's also developed a belief-system, which is that the world's governments are being controlled by cloud-people living in the sky above Chicago. For his cult to acquire legitimacy, however, the next stage must be to announce this news to the world by means of a grim and disgusting act of terrorism.

Philip's plan was to drop anthrax over Disneyland Paris with the aim of choking Mickey Mouse to death, and this would have been the horrifying scene to have greeted us this morning were it not for the fact that last night, at a Thai Restaurant in Ealing, the body of a forty-three-year-old man and five women aged between eighteen and twenty-two were found ritually slaughtered round a table, having deliberately overdosed on red and green chillis. No-one knows why the deaths occurred, although the head waiter later explained that, moments before, he'd just spoken to Philip Dawsons and told him that his cheque card was past its expiry date.

from 'THE MAN WHO MISTOOK
HIS BIKE FOR OLIVES'

I've worked five years now at the Neurology Park in Lausanne, and I still find myself gawping in fascination at the many disorders which peck at the brain like demented blue-tits. It's been my privilege to know scores of individuals with peculiar mental quirks and momentary snaps of the cortex which affect moving abnormalities in personal behaviour. I've written elsewhere of the woman who mistook insults for requests for salt (an otherwise healthy dame incapable of feeling emotional hurt but phenomenally generous with her seasoning). Some of you will also be familiar with my account of Thomas, the nine-year-old baker prodigy, and of Simone P, whose eyes rolled round by 180 degrees and who spent the last twenty years of her life looking at the inside of her head. You will have read my research on PK, the man who was allergic to being tall, on Mrs H, who could only live sideways, on Steven O'P, who confused childishness with banking, and Gerald H-Stevens who had a small hand-puppet lodged in the left side of his brain. However, since then I have come across further extravagances in cognitive behaviour, and I'm happy to set down here a couple of the best ones.

J was an advertising copywriter in a flourishing British firm. He was monied and successful, being the genius behind some brilliant advertising campaigns for asbestos. My first encounter with him indicates, though, the peculiar nature of his disorder. It was as I was driving across London one day. My windows were down, the air was fresh and Jackie Brambles was at her height. As I looked up, on a large billboard to the right of the road was something which couldn't fail to shake me to the gullet. It was a large advertising hoarding which said in big letters: 'Doctor, you must help me. Please ring this number.'

I did not have time to read the digits laid out beneath since at that moment the poster, which was on a revolving electronic billboard, swivelled into another one advertising mints for animals. However, as I rounded the corner I immediately spotted another perfectly sited poster saying, 'In case you missed that, the number again is 0171 298 7575.' Swiftly, I pulled in at a telephone kiosk and dialled. I got through to an advertising agency and was told that my prospective patient was unable to talk to me direct, but could I go visit him?

One hour later, in a large unpleasant lounge at the top of a glass tower in Holborn, and surrounded by giant billboards and marker pens, I met J and discovered the nature of his cerebral twist. For J was neurologically incapable of communicating other than through poster campaigns. My interrogation of him was painfully slow, since whenever I asked him a question he would pause momentarily to think of an answer and then book a series of poster sites across London, organize the printing and display of a sequence of placards illustrating his reply, and then send me off in my car. I would then have to do a circuit of central London before being able to come back to J for a subsequent question.

J was trapped in a ridiculous nether world of exclusively promotional experience. Subsequent studies showed the central communicative lobe of his brain to be severely damaged, all, that is, apart from the cortexes governing public visual projection and graphic design, which were hideously enlarged. This meant J had a flair for poster campaigns and sloganry, and it came as no surprise to discover that he'd been working in this field since the age of eleven. J was a brilliant advertising executive; in all other matters, though, he was an imbecile. There was very little I could do to help, though in time I made J's plight easier by linking him up, via a key-pad, to the neon billboard in Piccadilly

Circus, so that his conversation could at least be more easily located.

The diminution of the private and personal locuses within the brain, and the concomitant development of exclusively public cognitive structures of communication is not as unusual as one might expect. Another patient of mine, A, was only able to perform certain basic tasks such as washing and childbirth if she were famous. Somehow, the knowledge that she was known and photographed by millions of others was the only experiential reality which could act as a behavioural disinhibitor.

When famous, which she became as a result of the publication of my research about her, she was able to wash and have children. The tragedy was she could only care for these children in an extremely public manner, inviting press photographers in to the birth, and giving certain newspapers exclusive rights to the schooling. She lived her life totally for the mass market, and when her fame declined as the media turned their attention towards another patient of mine (a man who could burp tastes that were over twenty years old) she simply died, by choking on a camcorder.

This is a testimony to her interesting life.

LET'S GIVE THEM A BIG HAND-OUT

Quite rightly, there's a debate going on at the moment about how much people should get paid for doing highly responsible jobs. The massive pay increases given to chairmen of privatized utilities has provoked cries of condemnation and threats of assassination from leader writers and bishops alike, a sort of consensus on the matter which, it turns out, is disgustingly wrong. Our attitudes to the utilities chairmen would change for the better if we but knew the true extent of the responsibilities these terrific people have to carry.

Take Cedric Brown, the last Chief Executive of British Gas and a man who recently suffered a thousand impertinences for his receipt of a £475,000 salary. Yet he deserved all that money and more. Gas is a dangerous substance, as anyone knows who's had their scalp blown off by a faulty oven. It needs to be stored properly, and it was among Cedric Brown's many responsibilities each evening to look after any unused gas built in his factory and not sold that day. At night, the gas was driven from his office in a fleet of blue vans and then pumped into a specially sealed bedroom in his West London home. There it would remain under lock and key until the morning. Mr Brown therefore spent each night in the full knowledge that if he were to accidentally create a spark between 7 pm and 6 am, say by inadvertently stubbing his toe against something metal, or by punching someone wearing a neck brace, he and his entire family would end up as custard. It was a nerve-wracking and dangerous job, which Cedric gladly undertook so we might sleep safe from bits of stray gas.

The heads of the regional electricity boards put themselves under even more immediate danger. Each one of them, upon receipt of their £165,000 salary, must sign an undertaking to ensure the non-interruption of electrical flow throughout the regional grid irrespective of personal cost. So, for example, last winter Bryan Townsend, Chairman of Midlands Electricity, was called out to deal with a pylon cable that had snapped in two. By tethering one end of the cable to his foot and wrapping the other around his head, Mr Townsend used his body to complete the circuit, allowing twelve thousand volts per second to pass through it. Though his skin now has the exact texture of peeled walnut, his bravery did allow the entire population of Stafford to keep watching a particularly interesting edition of *Dangerfield* that evening. Yet Mr Townsend's courage still goes largely unsung.

Perhaps, though, this is as it should be. For it's a well kept fact that these men have contracted special super-powers through coming into repeated daily contact with powerful primeval forces such as gas and electricity. Cedric Brown's constant proximity to deadly gases has given him a heightened sense of smell, while Bryan Townsend's legs can act as capacitors. Both men have been dropped behind enemy lines on many occasions and used their super-powers to sniff out and recharge vital radar equipment. Together with Prison Service Director General, Richard Tilt, whose long experience of prison maintenance has given him the super-power to improvise cages out of any available material, including grass and windrushes, they've often been called upon to track down and incarcerate dangerous animals or escaped idiots.

Perhaps the most striking public duty, though, is performed by the chairmen of our water authorities, publicly castigated for drawing salaries of over £100,000 a year, but privately carrying out services beyond remuneration. We all know that being in charge of a water authority can be a dangerous, wet and backbreaking job, ensuring that the correct amount of liquid is sent to the correct tap whenever some is ordered up by a thirsty or dirty member of the public. For that alone, Sir Desmond Pitcher, Chairman of North West Water, deserves his £315,000 a year. But do you know that, to maintain the cleanliness of the water, Sir Desmond and his fellow chairmen have to swim regularly around in it, and sift it through their teeth to remove any gristle or impurities? Over the months, the regional water chairmen have evolved gills, webbed hands and water-resistant scaly skin to help them perform this function at ten-hour stretches without interruption. Today, these strange, mysterious men-fish, under their shoal-leader, Sir Frederick Holliday of Northumbrian Water, patrol the Atlantic and Irish sea beds, defending our shores from invasion by enemy submarines or basking sharks, while, for a small charitable donation, it's possible to swim with them in a safe pool by the Merseyside Development Corporation and feed them sprats.

Remember this before you curse them next. Then dig deep in your pockets, and give thanks for their public service.

THE GOD-HONEST TRUTH ABOUT CHRISTMAS

Until recently, practically all of us believed the New Testament account of the Nativity to be completely true. However, new evidence found by scientists and friends of scientists casts doubt on the miraculous nature of the story, and possibly spoils everything. The evidence is now well known, but here it is again.

1: The Star

Astronomers have spent thousands of years trying to come up with an acceptable theory about the movement of the planets and their cusps that would explain the references in the Nativity story to a Star in the East guiding the Wise Men to Bethlehem. Now it looks like they needn't have bothered. It seems that a simple mistranslation has corrupted our interpretation of the original text: the word 'star' is not, it's now claimed, referring to a celestial object but instead to a celebrity. So what the Wise Men found on their travels was a celebrity from the East who was travelling to Bethlehem at the time. Papyrus ticket stubs found in an Egyptian museum show that an Aramaic dancer called Menachem Habbakuk was touring about then, and it would have been highly unusual for his tour not to have taken in Bethlehem, then recognized as one of the Four Dance Regions of the Ancient World. All the Wise Men had to do then to find Bethlehem was follow posters.

2: The Wise Men

Work done recently by histo-sociologists proves that wise men didn't exist at that time. By cracking open fossilized skulls and colouring the rings in the brain, it's possible to tell how clever the skullees were. Studies show that levels of intelligence about two thousand years ago were so low as to be amusing. Men would spend most of their working day spitting, and for entertainment would compare the consistency of their spit with those of their companions. Women would mostly stay in the home, hiding from rocks and certain animals that looked like rocks. Nobody clever was born until well after the Crusades, and there were certainly no remotely wise men before then. It may be that the men referred to in the Nativity were simply alien spacemen.

3: The Stable

This certainly didn't exist, since most zoocheologists now believe that animals weren't discovered until 420 AD at the earliest. Before then, people farmed plants and buds, and hunted down wild bushes either for food or to tame as domestic pets. Most commercial establishments had outbuildings devoted to quite sophisticated methods of plant cultivation, so a more accurate translation of the Gospel original would be, 'There was no room for them at the Inn, so they slept in a nearby botanical garden.'

4: 'And they heard a host of heavenly angels singing "Behold, The King of Kings is born this day."'

There are three main inaccuracies in this text. Firstly, lexi-linguists tell us that the phrase 'Behold, The King of Kings is born this day' is most likely a misreading of an extremely similar Hebrew phrase meaning 'Behold, The King of Kings is not born this day.' The misreading occurred either in translation or, more likely, at the actual event itself, through mishearing what was being said.

This leads us to the second area of doubt, which is whether such a complex choir of voices could actually have been heard at all. Auro-sociologists tell us that the ability to hear in any great complexity did not develop until about the twelve hundreds, at about the same time as perspective was flourishing in the visual arts. Before then, it was more likely that people could hear no more than two-dimensionally, listening only to things coming from a straight line perpendicular to the sides of the head. Certainly, early ear muscles would have been unable to cope with a three deep choir, forty-five degrees up from the horizontal in the sky. It's more likely that the sound heard by the witnesses to the Nativity was someone whistling because he was happy, while the vision in the sky was either a cloud or alien spacecraft.

Certainly not angels. For here is perhaps the most startling finding. According to recent work done by psycho-biologists, angels did exist at that time, but not as heavenly beings. It seems clear now that a tribe of little four foot men, with stumps on their backs that were probably wing-relics from earlier in the evolutionary chain, did settle in Southern Jordan at around 40 BC, and angel droppings dating from then were found last month in a Gaza cave by a young terrorist boy. But it's also clear through evidence that these angels were scared of heights, so cannot be the ones referred to in the Nativity story singing in the sky. These were most likely some sort of shadow or maybe spacemen crashing.

In the face of all these findings, the whole matter should now be concluded once and for all.

A NEW WAY FORWARD FOR MOUTHS

Read my lips: no complex ideology communicated by elaborate and expansive phraseology.

For the task you and I face is a great one. It is not little, like a loganberry. Or a louse. It is not small, like a smear. It is immense. Momentous and mountainous. Horribly hilly.

The task I set out before you is simple. But then, simplicity and success can be promiscuous bedfellows. The task is this: to determine the meaning, to recognize the purport, to see the sense, and to identify the ultimate gist of what it is that is being said. Said not by us, but at us. Said from the mouth, by those whose mouths are public targets of our attention, and whose lips are two moving goalposts of substance.

Now, what do I mean by this? In many ways, I don't have to tell you. The evidence is there for all to see. It is there in the compactness. It is there in the, if you will, conciseness. A nice conciseness. A concise soundbiteness. Phrases are becoming shorter. The clause is extinct. There's no need for extras. All that baggage of argument. All that laundry of examination.

Now they give it to us straight. It makes things simpler. Easier to follow. Light exercise for the ears. Clarity of vision. Eardrum aerobics. Forward. A template for tomorrow. A completion of each sentence. In record time. More full stops since records began. A leaner lexicon. Ready for the Twenty-First Century. The challenges ahead. A thousand futures. A million possibilities. A billion perhapses.

We must learn to seize the perhaps. Together we can do such a thing. Bash the perhaps into a certainly. And then we can build on all our certainlies. Turn them into definitelies. And then we will begin the journey towards the foundation of a renewed communal victory in the land of yes, which can only be achieved through a commitment to the value of punchiness. And shortness.

And we each have a part to play. We each have a role to perform in this soundbite economy. For each one of us has the ability to hem in our phraseology. To cut back our adjectives and to get back to basic sentence structures. All that we want to say can be said swiftly in a simple slogan.

And that slogan is: tenacity and taciturnity are two sides of a powerful coin. Or, to put it another way: silence is golden, simplicity is silver, brevity is bronze. In other words: the shorter the line, the more we'll feel fine. That is: say it once, say it quickly, then stop. In effect: put up, then shut up. In short: we must be tough on presenting complex ideas in a non-simplistic way, and tough on the causes of presenting complex ideas in a non-simplistic way.

Once we grasp this truth, then all other truths become self evident. Become a thousand points of light in the candelabra of certainty. Once again, in one axiom, we will be able to couple the past and the future, the here and now, the rich and the poor, the haves and the have-nots, the young and the old, the cow jumped over the moon.

Listen to me. These words are important. Decency. Honesty. Community. Energy. Hospitality. Brie. Society. Civility. Chimney. They form the nexus of a bedrock of an agenda. Out of these words, through the alchemy of hope and the Mephistopheles of partnership, we will transform our society into one in which everyone has equal fun.

Of course, it will not be easy. There will be those who say 'It cannot be done. With the best will in the world, you cannot make a crystal horse out of damp soot.' But I say to those Jeremiahs amongst us who would do down our hopes, and throw sponges at our dreams, I say to them: 'Look not on what is there, but on what should be there.' Or, to put it simply: 'Ask not for a bit of give and take, but take a bit then ask to give. And say: 'What I do for my country, I do for my country.' That is what I say to them.

So how can we achieve this total understanding? How can we reach down and tug at the giblets of what is being said? How can we scare off the baboons of confusion? Well, we can start by listening. But listening deafly. Beyond the annoyance of the literal understanding of words, lies a greater prize. The selective understanding of words. By adopting the principle of selection, by discriminating between good basic words and disastrously complex ones, we can once again empower ourselves as individuals with the freedom to choose what we would like to hear.

By liking what we hear, and responding well to what is being said, we are perfecting our roles as responsible citizens of the New Britain. Our intelligence enables us to cut through the coagulating mists of too many words and applaud the clarity and precision, the double whammy, of their slogans.

So let us then go forward. To go backwards would be a reversal. And let us affirm our commitment to this new deal in political partnership. If they promise to speak simply to us, then let us promise to behave simply by accepting what they say with minimum fuss. That is, quite literally, the very least we can do.

And let us begin today. For there is much work to be done, and the task is a great one. Not small, like a skunk. But huge, like a hot air balloon. It is a task which you and I have to face together. Only together can we tackle it; for, if we are apart, it will tackle us. One at a time. One. By. One. Going. For. The. Legs.

A SWITCH IN TIME

A few months ago a man came to my door. He carried a briefcase in a colour I hadn't seen before and which I've never managed to identify since, despite careful searches through most of the nation's reference libraries and swatch directories. Apart from that, he looked perfectly normal, the sort of man you'd expect to turn up at your house with an armful of crazy-paving brochures or, at a push, leaflets on Mormonism and the joys of tea celibacy.

I was expecting a religious presentation as soon as I heard his first words: 'Sorry to disturb you, but I wonder if I could talk to you about some of the ways you spend your life?'

'I think you're wasting your time,' I said, not keen on squandering another half-hour stood in a door-step puddle rebuffing claims from a smiling person that Catholics were harlots.

'Ah no, I think you're the one wasting your time,' he replied. 'About 44% of it.'

'I'm sorry?'

'44% of your time is wasted. You know you should always leave your car keys by the phone when you come in, but you don't, so every morning about three and a half minutes is spent looking for them. You dawdle around the bakery section of Tescos for five and three quarter minutes, even though you know you always end up buying sliced white. You tried to develop an interest in kites and spent three weekends on an inappropriately elevated common manufacturing enjoyment in a project which you later admitted was just a spurious attempt to tell your doctor you do plenty of exercise. Add to this the fourteen months spent taking that route home along Anderson Street before you discovered the short cut down Monks Lane and across Widney Grove, the three years' Latin you did at school, and all the novels and television and films you've seen and read which you didn't like, always knew you wouldn't like but read and watched anyway because other people talked about them and you wanted to talk about them too but which you ended up never talking about because you couldn't bring yourself to say you didn't like them. Add that day you got lost and walked a nine-mile tetrahedron around Dumfries, and the two years you lived in Greenock as a boy and failed to develop emotionally or intellectually by any significant degree. Add also the seconds you spend just standing and staring at objects around the house when you're meant to be making a decision about cooking, add the moments when you stop everything because you think you're going to sneeze but you don't sneeze, or the day those grapes made you sick, and you'll find that approximately 44% of your life is spent on activities that have no material or spiritual reward, lead to a negligible enrichment of your person, and generate so minimal an amount of memorable experience as to prove by any applied definition to be an absolute and total waste of your time.'

'You'd better come in,' I said, trying not to look as if someone had just rammed a hand down my throat and slapped my soul about a bit. 'But how did you get all this information?'

'Guess work. You can probably rely on everyone having at least three of those examples apply to them at some stage. You'll be surprised at the number of people who've taken up kiting recently.'

'Right, and you've come here to show me how I can enrich my life by looking at St Mark's Gospel and giving up Earl Grey have you?'

'No, no. I've come to show how much money you could make from your life if you sold it.'

'Sold it?'

'Yes. Well, bits of it anyway. The bits you waste.'

The man came in, sat down and opened his mysteriously tinted suitcase while I stood passively in my living room like a stuffed bear. Over the hours, he took me through leaflets and application forms which have subsequently changed my life (although almost halved it). Let me explain. Each one of us carries a 44% unused life. This spare time is of enormous value to certain exceptional individuals who actually find themselves so busy that they literally don't have enough hours in the day, or who are rich enough to buy up pieces of spare time as an investment. To them, our unused time acquires a value, and one which we should be encouraged to realize by selling off. The only downside would be that, technically, some of our time would then be owned by someone else, so that, for example, certain selected bits of life would have to be spent running the transportation office of someone else's coffee packaging firm or being a vocalist in a slightly over-hyped Calypso-Techno crossover band from Auckland.

But once we've made money from sold time, we can then afford to buy into the unused lives of other people who participate in the Life-Sharing scheme. So, I discovered from the stranger's time-chart that fifty-two hours of my life buys me an hour of Ken Russell's, although it would be of Ken Russell when he wasn't doing anything. A week gets me a minute's sleepy Barbara Taylor Bradford.

I signed up instantly, sold off all my wasted time (which to my delight I discovered to be higher than average, at 62%) and now surf the likes of Jack Straw when he has a head-cold and, occasionally, Tom Hanks at a bad opera. In return, my spare moments have been bought up by an anonymous American time-stock conglomerate, which is why I'm writing this on the night-flight to Chicago, where I'm about to spend the next fourteen weeks in their vaults. I'd get out of this scheme, but unfortunately the man at the door with the abnormally pigmented suitcase has proved too busy to be contacted.

HISTORY

I've just returned from an academic conference at Aston University held to determine the shape of history. The general conclusion was that it's cyclical, but some minority papers were published by Professor Norman Stone of Oxford University (who says history is tubular) and Hugh Trevor Roper (who thinks it's shaped like a horn). Sir Isaiah Berlin, always an original thinker, said that history has no shape but does smell of pear. He also said that history is when time looks in a mirror, but he was just shouted down for being clever.

The most emotionally charged moment of the whole three-day session came towards the end. As assorted historians, biographers, archivists, brass rubbers, hagiographers, and war enthusiasts showered insults on each other during the closing vote to determine the most popular date, the brawling pamphleteers were quelled by an impassioned cry from an old man at the back, sitting in the non-academic seats, who spoke directly but profoundly:

'History!' he said. 'You ask what is history? I can't walk more than a hundred yards from my house. Anything beyond a hundred yards is history. My present-day stops at the ironmonger's. I can't chew my meat any more. My gums are like two burst balloons. I must buy ready-chopped foods only. For me, a whole cutlet is history. I cannot stand for more than sixty minutes without wanting to relieve myself. Therefore, I can never again queue at a book-signing session for popular authors. I can only have books signed by unpopular authors. Like you. My home is now littered with unwanted signed first editions of your works, and at night I stumble over unnecessary introductions to French Radicalism on my way to the toilet bowl. In my last years I am surrounded by idiocy. Idiocy! Idiocy! That is history!'

With that, he immediately collapsed to applause and became a popular cultural icon.

As the end of the millennium approaches, it's important we make some final decisions about our sense of perspective. That's why I leapt at the chance to attend this historic meeting of great minds as they contemplated a thousand events and tried to make everything we've ever done look deliberate. (The meeting itself can only now be described as historic following a hotly contested vote in the opening session.) I wanted to see how they would handle the utter randomness of our doings and go about choosing the best ones for the Greatest Hits album planned for release as the aeon comes to a close. I also wanted to catch up on the latest trends in historical analysis, and so spent a day wandering around the different history stalls each visiting professor had erected in the Exhibition Tent.

The Social History Counter was the busiest. The drift away from straightforward chronological accounts of the doings of kings and presidents and towards the examination of the underlying currents of social practice within communities and cultures drew big crowds. Here was where the action was. Dr Philip Clockerty of Miriam's University, Wisconsin was selling copies by the score of his paper on 'The Dropping of the Atom Bomb and Its Effect on Housing Conditions in mid-Twentieth Century Hiroshima'. To his left, Oliver Stone, formerly a cinematic biographer of the likes of Kennedy and Nixon, could now be seen signing a multi-million dollar Hollywood deal to bring out a movie version of traditional patterns of husbandry in Elizabethan rural England. Anthony Hopkins' name had been touted as a hoe.

Other scholars were also enormously active, selling histories individually tailored by specialist markets. In a small booth, Professor

Strum Thorsen was outlining his projected 'History Of Embarrassment', starting in 1310 with Bavarian novice monk, Brother Jürgen,
the first man to discover he could not urinate within the sight of other
men. Next to him, Lord David Stetson was presenting a paper on
'History For Dogs', concentrating on the smells and colourful shapes
that raged for three days during the Battle of Waterloo.

But the greatest excitement came from the mouth of Professor Barry
Shostakovitch, head of the respected research centre the Massachusetts
Truth Factory, who outlined his newly published views on the meaning
of history. He argued that we generate a sense of history out of a
mental attempt to forestall our awareness of the passage of time.
Confronted with the inevitability of our own bodily decay, we construct
a much more durable body of history, into which we place our lives
in a futile and laughable attempt to make them look more significant.
Unfortunately, this procedure only works if we've ever been a king or
a screen goddess. Since this traditional mechanism of history so often
failed to score for the mass of insignificant individuals who were taught
it, Shostakovitch argued, excitedly, it was now time to propose a new,
more upbeat approach to historical analysis. He then proceeded to
outline, while dribbling, a feelgood model of history which left his
audience roaring with optimism.

It was an attempt to forestall our sense of mortality by producing a
history that concentrated on starts rather than finishes. The conclusions
of events were ignored, to give the impression they might still be
happening. Over the course of the next three hours, Shostakovitch
produced, while perspiring like a horse, a cheerful account of beginnings throughout the last two thousand years, starting with the birth
of Christ, and going on to narrate the separate birth dates of the early
Christian martyrs. He described the start of the Hundred Years War,
but refused to say when it ended or how long it took. Napoleon's
invasions of Western Europe and Northern Africa were outlined
obliquely through references to where his troops invaded from (in all

cases, France). His book stops just before the Second World War, at 1868 and the conception of Neville Chamberlain.

Shostakovitch is now planning a companion volume, which outlines man's major sporting achievements over the last hundred years, giving an exhaustive account of the start times of all successful world record attempts.

I left the conference excited but troubled. Questions raged in my head that needed answering. Have we made too much history? What if we've got the order wrong? I determined to explore the whole horrible subject further and construct my own much better theory of how history works. I came across some interesting nuggets of knowledge in my research.

Firstly, I discovered that in about 946 BC, two competing civilizations decided to have a history race. The Mycenean civilization of Southern Syracuse and the y-Boki Empire of West China met up and arranged to found themselves at the same time, but in different hemispheres. They agreed to run over the course of the next thousand years and see who produced the most history before dying out. The only two rules were that each civilization would expand in territory but must not stray into the other's hemisphere, and that any dying out before the allotted thousand years would automatically be construed as a unilateral withdrawal from the competition and would be met with a heavy fine.

Amidst great excitement, the founding fathers of both civilizations lined up on the equator at the start of 946 BC, blew a horn and then began migrating. Sixty years later, they were all recalled because of a false start. The horn was blown again, and the race proper commenced. The y-Boki blasted out the traps, reaching China by 852 BC, but the Myceneans got bogged down fashioning earthen pots and constructing a system of pig deities before they had travelled 50 kilometres south. (Though the pots later helped them pick up points for presentation.) In 858 BC, although neither civilization had yet developed fundamental weaponry, the quickly settled y-Boki people grew cocky and began decorating ostrich eggs. This was to prove their undoing, since ostrich eggs proved notoriously difficult to pigment, and the development of gold leaf overlay techniques took them the best part of four hundred years. By this time, the Myceneans quickly caught up by being suddenly wiped out in battle by Alexander The Great in 342 BC. Though they now no longer existed, this event was deemed more historic than anything the y-Boki had ever done with their eggs, and was declared a technical knockout.

Another discovery has enabled me to trace history back to its source. This occurred exactly 2,349,445 years ago. Up until then, for about a million years prior to this, history could not be measured because all events were insignificant. The Earth was populated by tribes of peoples who lacked self-confidence and thought it best not to get involved. They kept themselves to themselves, and were scared of doing anything different in case others might think it made them look foolish.

However, 2,349,445 years ago all this changed when a Paleolithic man did the first significant thing. While out hunting, he disagreed with his tribal leader over the projected whereabouts of a herd of bison. In that one instant, the man brought into the world the primitive beginnings of factionalism, deductive reasoning, initiative, constitutional theory, and map reading. Unable to persuade the others in the tribe, the man went off by himself. But found nothing. It turned out the tribal leader had been right after all, and the man later had to apologize for doubting him and was made to eat poisoned shin. After this incident, no-one dared raise any more questions for another thirty-four thousand years, but the discordant seeds of upset had been sown.

Armed with this important information, I have attempted to produce a history of all things. It takes into account fresh discoveries which will fundamentally transform our understanding of many previously familiar narratives. (For example, it's now clear that the early American

Pioneers first trekked to the West in search of yams.) So, I will be able to reveal that the first Christians were extremely rude, known throughout the Roman Empire for their repetitive belches and insults, and for their frequent habit of walking along the streets and just banging into people instead of skirting around them. Convinced they were protected by God, the early Christian community went around Europe making remarks about baldness, and laughing at people's stammers. Recent evidence suggests that the fate of many of them in the Colosseum may have been justified.

Other discoveries have shown that Genghis Khan fought all his wars by correspondence, delivering his tactical manoeuvres by letter to each enemy while staying in Mongolia, and then allowing several months for them to write back a reply. Wars would rage in the post throughout northern Asia, until eventually Genghis, a keen letter writer, built up an Empire via the mail system.

I also have evidence that the Sumatrans were the first Empire to take a six month sabbatical.

I have used as my source material the enormous pile of unstudied marginalia in ancient documents which previous historians have discarded as pointless doodles but which I have now established are none other than a vast series of personal memos. Whole cave interiors dating back to the Neolithic era contain obscure boar's blood pigmentations of quick messages these ape-like creatures would scrawl as reminders to themselves not to forget to damp their fires at night and get more flint in by the next hunt. A whole cave in Southern France contains a twenty-foot-high list of shopping provisions, while woven into the Bayeux Tapestry is the message 'Get milk for Friday'. It may be that the rocks of Stonehenge form a complex memo pad reminding someone from that area that he needs to talk to Peter, and some Egyptian Pyramid hieroglyphics have been translated as 'show Tuten big rm and kp fish fr Tuesday' which no-one has been able to make any sense of.

I've also been studying people's attitudes to the passing of time. In the past, no-one would complain if it took four hundred years to build a stone cathedral. Today, we ask for compensation if our water taps are not repaired by nightfall. Have we lost the sense of the unimportance of passing time? Are we currently incapable of thinking in decades? An initial survey reveals that in the first millennium AD, when life expectancy was so short, people thought most things were a waste of time since they knew they would never live to see them completed anyway. So they couldn't be bothered doing them quickly. Most cathedrals could actually have been built then in about three years if everyone put their back into it, but such was the plague of sluggishness which dominated that time, that people got used to the concept of slowness (records reveal it was the only thing taught at centres of learning) and it became the norm for it to take five hours to wake up and fourteen days to clean a pig. The first Olympic Games in Athens took a year, though they had only one event, the Triple Jump. (It's believed that five-day Test Cricket is a modern-day relic of these times.)

From everything I had so far studied, it became clear that our notions of what is and is not historic are entirely subjective. If this is the case, though, it may be possible we can trace back to the brain the mechanism which distributes 'significance', and see whether it is applied randomly to events. To this end, I built a laboratory and placed some people in there from birth. I made them grow up without any sense of history and forbade them from having traditions. Eventually, they thought everything they did was being carried out for the first time. One of them published a paper on opening a jar of coffee, while four of them organized a conference to examine the decline of cereal consumption in the period dating from the advent of lunch. All of them elected each other to lucrative fellowships set up to research changes in their own social structure between 5 and 9 pm each day.

It was clear from my experiment that man carries within him an innate and annoying capacity to historicize. What was frightening here, though, was the evidence that his historicizing was arbitrary, and that the likes of wars, political reforms and terrific inventions, what we have always regarded as significant, may in fact be no more or less critical than a fly in a stadium.

So does objective significance exist? During further research I was able to measure objectively how much significance each participant placed on an event (which I did scientifically, by asking them), and from these findings I was able to calculate backwards to arrive at a retrospective objective evaluation of the event itself. I then applied this rubric to the mass of events which have so far made up the present century, and correlated it with the rate of change of levels of significance within time.

My conclusion is startling and may win me a prize. It proves that a thousand years from now what will be regarded as the single most important event of the last hundred years is the decision of a Lapland cattle herder in 1929 to move his herd from the tundra around Lake Inari in Finland to the plains of Lainio in Sweden. At the end of the next millennium no-one will be interested in de Gaulle, the Tokyo Olympics or chemical warfare (though the one musical influence they will still recognize is that of the Troggs). Bigger wars will have taken the place of the first two World ones. Greater achievements will have superseded the advent of the hovercraft and the cement mixer. As the dust of our bones settles in the earth, herder Bulen Hari's fateful decision to shepherd his cattle westwards will remain profoundly respected, initiating, as it will, a copy-cat movement of livestock across the north, the decline of Russian land values, the Finnish Civil War and the eleven-hundred-year rule of the Lappish Empire.

Applying my method to all previous history, I have been able to identify only three other dates of equal objective significance.

The first is 892 BC, when the Greeks invented truth and tried it out on small colonial outposts in Sicily. With the advent of truth, fixed certainties came to dominate daily existence, and a lot of fun disappeared from people's lives because they could no longer make things up and pass them off as fact. The first to suffer were the Carthaginians, whose entire empire turned out to be a lie. Once the Carthaginians were discovered to have been making things up, the vast Mediterranean territories they had been claiming to have controlled for three centuries simply disappeared.

The next important date is 1205 AD, when the last surviving Nordic god started up a whale farm just outside Reykjavik. This signalled a final and decisive abandonment of spirituality in favour of the claims of purely temporal human experience, and led to the steady emasculation of religious authority culminating in the terrible martyrdom of the Grated Nuns of Innsbruck in 1698.

And finally, all man's behaviour and thought changed radically after 1402, when the world's first burglary was committed. This event totally overturned all notions of property and ownership, and led to the development of the twin institutions of law and fences.

There are currently no other dates worth knowing.

But no history of all things can be concluded without addressing that single, most important and uniquely inevitable of dates, the end of time itself. One would think it might be possible to calculate this date more or less precisely using our superior knowledge of the physical universe and its patterns of behaviour measured against the rate of expansion of the galaxies. But this would be to ignore the unconquerable evidence of my already legendary research, which has proven a direct link between events and man's subjective imagination.

For the awful truth is that man shapes time in his own image, and that things happen as we would want them to be, including the end of time. More particularly, this means the world will end in a very human way. Time will not stop. It will simply go into retirement.

All my evidence suggests that the end of the world will be signalled by people taking up hobbies, putting their financial affairs in order, selling all their furniture and booking into sheltered accommodation.

This will happen on a global scale. A furniture glut will spread around the world, leading to a drop in the price of mahogany and the cessation of rainforest clearances, which will in turn lead to a fatal imbalance in the eco-system. Inner cities from Helsinki to Brisbane will become derelict, as vast populations move out to newly constructed leafy suburbs and coastal resorts, leaving the centre of each country to develop into expanding desert wildernesses. Eventually, the entire population of the planet will have booked into its sheltered housing, and the visiting relative will become extinct. As the end draws near, the people of the world will gather round a piano at night and sing songs. Then eight hundred billion people will go to bed at a quarter-past-nine. These people will include vast business conglomerates, governments, economists, and historians, all of them in slippers. Companies like Shell will book into a small place in Shropshire, carrying on its business at first, more as a hobby than anything else, then gradually winding down its operations as its Central Control Division's mind starts to wander. Within a year of the end of time, it will not be able to remember anything about oil, and will have trouble retaining even the simplest price negotiations in its head.

Eventually, time will end with prime minister and property developers, heads of state and hairdressers, kings and contact lens suppliers confusing memories of the past and present, and babbling incoherently about someone they once loved. And soon, no-one will have the faintest idea what anything means any more.

And it is at that point, that history will be deemed to have stopped. Except, there will be no-one around capable of deeming it.

MEN: AN ORAL HISTORY OF MEN

MEN: An oral History of Men

Testimony 1: Billy Bobson (a man, born in 1921).

'Course, you had to fight in those days. It was expected of you, if you was a man. You was expected to be a good fighter and all, Bantamweight Champion of the World, something like that. I remember I went down the local shipyards looking for irregular work, and they was only taking on successful Bantamweights. So I lied, and said I'd won a title fight, and I forged some newspaper headlines with me photograph in them showing me gaining the title in Las Vegas, and I faked some commentary, and they believed me, so they took me on. My job was, I had to fight any new ships that were built the previous week. As soon as the ship was ready, they'd wheel her out in the yard, and all the other men would crowd round her in a circle, and I'd get me gloves on, and I'd have to fight her. All the men would shout 'Come on, Billy, give her one!' 'Mind her keel!' that sort of thing, though some of the bosses would be cheering on the ship, shouting 'Come on, Queen Mary! He's only a man. Trap his ankle underneath you!' They was good natured fights but, oh, some of them could be really fatal.

Testimony 2: Clive Snippers (a heavy man, born in 1934).

We men were not allowed to show emotions in those days. The only emotion we were allowed to show was a sort of cynical laugh at others' folly. Apart from that, all other emotions were confiscated from us when we were three. On our third birthday, we were shown into a new room in the house, and left for an hour and told to empty all our emotions in it. Then an hour later our parents would come back, remove us, lock the room, and hand the key over to the local doctor or to some other professional, and that key would never be seen again.

So we had to express our emotions in secret, so I remember a lot of adult men like my father would meet together in a small clump in the woods outside our town, and there they would dance and frolic, and have skipping contests and all cry together at the beauty of oak trees. Then they would come home that night, and say they were drunk and wanted to beat our mothers up, but they never would because you could see they were secretly tender, and still had moss on their shoes, so all they could do was sort of cynically laugh at others' folly. And that is why no men at that time had any respect from children.

Testimony 3: Michael Ignatieff (a bright man, born in 1949).

You were never allowed to be clever just after the War. If you read a book or liked colours you was regarded as sissy or a 'fay-donkey' and you were pelted with garish cloths by all the other children. I remember I told my father I wanted to join a library and he vomited on me a whole day. It just wasn't manly to be clever, so we had to pretend to be stupid all the time, and bump into things, and touch hot wires accidentally and say, 'Oh, I didn't think, but I'm alright anyway, the electrocution didn't hurt me too much, I can take it.'

And all the boys had pissing games, where we'd piss and piss and piss and see who could piss the thickest, and then we'd laugh at piss, and say our piss was the best piss, and that was how we were meant to spend our time, but me and my mates would secretly leave the other boys and go off into our den behind my dad's workshop and play Truth and Value games. We were known as the Truth and Value gang, and we'd have fights with some of the other secret intellectual gangs in the neighbourhood, like the Fleetwood Epistemologists who met down the road, who were nine-year-old hard nuts really, but had some interesting ideas about the definition of Meaning which I later used in one of my novels.

Testimony 4: Steven Steiner (a gay man, born gay in 1937).

It was very different being gay men in those days, because for one thing, since you didn't have any emotions you didn't really know you were gay, and you could maybe spend your whole life being gay but not actually being aware of it. The other thing was that men regarded women as a bit feckless, and boys never went with girls because they had ridiculous soft hands and feet, and you was a 'fay-buzzard' if you was seen playing near a girl, and our fathers told us to keep away from them in case we catched Girl. So, in those days it was far more manly to go out for the evening with a man in a dress, because that proved you didn't hang out near women because the person in a dress you were with was obviously a hairy man, which was alright. So lots of men in those days would dress up in ladies' clothing, and parade around the town centre, and other men would go up to them and say 'Excuse me, lady-man, would you go with me for the evening?'

But I suppose I was different because I was gay, so I got away with hanging out with girls and women, and I would spend lots of time in their company, and have fun and penetration and things like that, and I was regarded as being gay and a 'fay-branagh' and men would laugh at me, and it was a terrible affliction.

Testimony 5: Sandy Holbein (a tall man, born 1943).

You were expected to be good with your hands then, and I remember once I was making my wife a large box for her oil and as I was making it I accidentally nailed my arm to the inside. I was losing blood pretty quickly, but I didn't really want to say anything in case other men laughed at me for not being able to make boxes without injury, so I kept quiet and stayed there attached to the box. After a while, I knew I was gangrenous but I didn't really want to go to the doctor's because, you know, you don't really want to talk about rotting flesh because that sort of thing is private, so I just kept quiet and hoped it would sort itself out. So, I was inside the box for twenty days, getting weaker and weaker, and my wife eventually threw the box out, not knowing I was inside it. I didn't say anything to her at the time because we didn't really say much to each other after we were married, so the box was taken off to a crusher and it was only then that someone noticed and said, 'Hold on, that's Sandy Holbein in that box!' and they tried to pull me out and I said, 'Don't bother, I'm alright thanks,' but they pulled me out anyway, and now my life has been hell because of all the teasing I've had from my mates for the last forty years. I really wish I'd been born a girl.

THIS WOODEN 'NO-NO'

A lot of people think that the theatre is, of all artistic experiences, the worst. This is on the basis it's the one most prone to serving its audiences a succession of expensive though subsidized disappointments. These same people say that there's nothing more appalling on God's Earth or even Satan's Hell than being trapped in front of a long, bad play, especially if it's one about the conflict between memory and shifting power structures within a family coming to terms with their butler's autism. They argue that the views afforded by the seats in most of Britain's theatres are little short of obscene jokes targeted against the ability to see, and claim that no single play has ever been as good as its poster. Astonishment is the best they can muster at the realization that so much time and effort has been expended by the wasted, starving bodies of fourteen actors, forty-three cynical back-stage staff, an out-of-control set designer, a double-booked costume fitter and a confused director who can't decide whether the play is about oppression or about transport, to come up with what is essentially some running around in a house with a lot of balconies so that the public can see a man who's been in a pasta commercial.

Not only that, but the temporary nature of theatre makes the whole absurd exercise twice as pointless. Sets are pulped and cast fed to the dole-queues when the eight-week run is up, Dame Helen slumps in a spa in a Swiss steam-room while one lucky actor gets another appearance fee in an ad. for Colman's Linguini. That's it. No monuments, no videos, no replays. All gone. Memories and air. Surely it's a rubbish way to behave. Theatre is a stinking, wretched art form peopled by inflated ingrates who criminally waste our lives. To hell with it.

However, I don't subscribe to this view. I love theatre. I love its traditions and camaraderie, I love what it does to the soul, I love the electric charge of livid peril that each night threatens for both actor and audience. I love its big sweaty bath of affection.

For the last eight years I've turned my spare energies to making theatre an essential part of absolutely everyone's everyday life. I started my own company, the Erotic Curtain, while still on a student grant and have since built it up into a three thousand dollar industry. The plays we put on then were disturbing and unpopular, and I was consequently signed up to direct a whole season at the Royal Court. That 1992 winter was memorable because for all three plays, *The Merry Wives of Windsor*, *Habeas Corpus*, and *Peter Pan*, I focused on just one metaphor, that of incontinence. There were highs and lows during that season (an example of a high: the uplifting determination and commitment to her craft that Juliet Stevenson displayed drinking ten pints of Pepsi each night before going on to give a magnificent Captain Hook. Some lows? *The Merry Wives of Windsor* being closed due to flooding, and the bill for the cost of replacing most of the Royal Court's electrical wiring.)

On reflection, it was probably a good thing that I left mainstream theatre that year under a cloud of unsurpassed hatred and threats of violence from Lord Gowrie, because it gave me the opportunity to think about what I really wanted to do with the nature of Performance and her sister, Shock. Since then I have resolutely stuck to my conviction that theatre and life should mirror each other exactly. To this end, in 1994 I mounted the first of my now legendary Copernican Evenings. Inspired by the old astronomer Copernicus' discovery that the Earth was not at the centre of the universe, but actually quite a bit off to one side revolving around the sun, I applied his crucial physical discoveries to my own productions, piling the audience into the stalls of a London theatre but staging the action exactly fifty-four miles away. Each night, I revolved the performers a further thirteen degrees in an anti-clockwise circle fifty-four miles from the theatre. The season was a triumph, and I received only four assaults. One night had to be cancelled, when the cast hit a reservoir.

This year, I've been aiming to turn life into theatre. All last week I sent my neighbours a series of reviews of their lives and asked them to post them up outside their houses. Most of them obliged, including Mrs Davies whom I described as 'disappointing', the Colinson family, who emerged as 'triumphantly resurrecting banality into an art form' and the occupants of Dr Katz's surgery, who were 'turgid'. I also sent flowers to a computer sales manager called David Starkey on the day of an important presentation he was giving to a client from Holland, wishing him good luck on its opening, and for the last four weeks I've always made a point of waiting outside Mr Starkey's office and applauding as he comes out at the end of the day. I've also collected the autographs of everyone who works for McVitie's Biscuits.

Perhaps my most ambitious undertaking is the campaign I'm currently running to persuade the Government to change the country to British Theatre Time. Most people are unaware that actors sleep during the day and are constantly looking for something to eat at eleven o'clock at night. By the time they've finished, there aren't any buses and some of them get killed walking home to their girl-friend's flat. So far, I've got David Hare, Steven Berkoff and Roger Daltrey to sign my petition asking for clocks on the mainland to be moved forward eleven hours so that children can go to school in the winter along roads safely illuminated by theatre lights and actors can have a decent lunch.

If that fails, then we'll surely succeed in our back-up proposal, which is to have a network of special buses laid on for actors at 6 pm and midnight each night, picking them up and dropping them off at their theatres and girlfriends' flats so that no-one need worry again about the risks they run braving each trip to the theatre on their own. Julie McKenzie has agreed to drive the Highgate bus. That's why I love her. She's a trooper. And has a clean licence.

INFANT LEAVES

It's probably time to give my opinion on some of the most recent books for children, concentrating mainly on review copies that have been sent to me free.

Starting with toddlers, you may find Hubert Angina's *Little Tommy Towel* keeps them smiling for a minute or so. It's a vivaciously illustrated short book about the adventurers of a small hand-towel normally used to clean the faces of kids Jill and Hugh but which is sometimes incorrectly borrowed by their father, Mr Liam Patterson. Your children will also get to know other delightful hygiene-oriented characters in these tails, such as Laticia The Sink, Bert Pumice, the wise old Professor Lillette, and Hairy Ann, the Fat Lavatory Brush [£3.99, Junior Olive Press. Also available by the same author, *Freddy Fax-Modem Goes To The Zoo*].

Four-year-olds and upwards beginning to take an interest in music may enjoy *The Puffin Book of Jazz*, the perfect introduction to this popular free-form rhythmical style. Chapters on Scatt and Swing take your children through the basics of improvisation, while they can also have fun cutting out and dressing their own trumpeters [£6.99, Papsy Stoddard Publications].

Fun With Onions is a fact book for nine-year-olds. It answers most of the questions kids normally ask parents about onions, and is packaged with attractive and immense illustrations which will help even the most inquisitive child understand the intricate workings of this mysterious vegetable. There's an onion workbook to accompany the publication, in which the author claims 'Even the parents may learn something new about onions!' Shallots are also covered [£4.50, Children's Husbandry Press].

While we're looking at educational books, *The Pop-Up Book of The Dead* is highly recommended. Aimed at the ten and eleven market, it provides perhaps the best introduction to what can sometimes be an emotive and embarrassing subject. A talking corpse takes your child through twenty different types of death, from the passing on of household pets to sudden cardiac arrests among grown-ups, while the index covers most carcinogens. The book is part of a series designed to steer your child's emotional development towards a clearer understanding of real situations. Forthcoming titles will include *The Pop-up Book of Toxic Waste, Where Does Internal Haemorrhaging Come From?*, and *The World of John Pilger* [£5.99, The Jarvis Cocker Unit].

For young adults (eleven to twelve-year-olds) Susan Tracks has brought out another well-written and never patronizing love story with *Julie's Fellatio Summer* [£7.50, Harrison Birtwhistle Press]. Julie is fourteen and belongs to a nine-parent family in Leicester. Naturally, the summer holidays are filled with the nauseous tedium associated with living in that area, and the summer of 1990 looks as if it will be no different. That's until she meets Timothy the Idiot, a local clown from a nearby circus troupe which specializes in coaxing llamas onto trapezes. Timothy takes Julie to see him perform, and, as they get to know each other, introduces her to his clowny way of life. Soon she is much more interested in running about in baggy trousers and driving a small car that collapses than she ever was in her Geography GCSEs. As the new term approaches, Timothy the Idiot offers her a part in his act (being attacked by badgers in a circus-animal recreation of the Normandy landings) and Julie has to choose between life in Leicester or life on the road as a performing buffoon. Her decision may surprise you, but read what happens for yourself in this sensitively written story about the complexities of an everyday relationship between girl and clown.

For thirteen to fourteen-year-olds there's another visit to the fantasy land of Anorexia in Keith Lopsicle's *The Further Chronicles of Thin City* [£5.00, Discarded Sweetmeats Publishing]. In this novella, the travelling starship of beautiful thin people outcast from Planet Earth are appalled by the sight on their radar screens of a massive sun. Measuring forty thousand miles in diameter, it is judged by the Narrow Council governing the ship to be too fat for investigation, and so is destroyed by nuclear weapons. Unfortunately, the blast releases a mysterious cloud of cholesterol which partially infects the ship and makes everyone put on an ounce. The only way the gaunt pioneers can save themselves is by hurling forward in time to 3 Million AD, when the universe starts to contract, and spend thirty-eight years there losing an ounce each. An allegory.

Finally, for fifteen-year-olds comes *Waste The Elderly: An End To Generation Overload* [Free, Her Majesty's Internet], a junior political pamphlet now secretly circulating on-line in school technology classes. The pamphlet calls for the setting up of an independent homeland for children under the age of sixteen, where their vastly superior knowledge and command of technology can be allowed to flourish in an economy unhampered by adult ignorance. The preferred option is for the children's state to be established by purely democratic means, but the writers are under no illusions that, since this is unlikely to occur in their lifetime (a lifetime now being redefined as seventeen years), an electronic uprising may have to take place. The authors set out their plans to destabilize the mature world by hacking into life-support systems in city hospitals and upsetting the equilibrium of anyone over thirty-five.

Happy reading, and mind that child.

THE PEACE THAT FAKETH
ALL UNDERSTANDING

Syvanos y Craxton is 80 this week. Still in formidable health, this most famous of Canadian-Moroccans remains devoted to the cause of peace, a lifelong endeavour which has justly seen him rewarded with five Nobel Peace Prizes, two Cubes du Gloire from Presidents Pompidou and Mitterand, and one of twelve Extended Gandhi Kisses distributed by Elizabeth Taylor in 1985. Syvanos has worked tirelessly for peace in El Salvador, Honduras, Syria, Montenegro, Switzerland, and Bath. His Foundation for the Prevalence of Accord has offices in a hundred and forty international trouble spots, with planning applications lodged in a further thirty-eight.

Syvanos himself has a slight, modest appearance, with a stooped back, small frame and mottled, ugly face. Close friends say he has dainty legs. To this day, he works tirelessly in the cause of peace, writing letters to presidents and prime ministers and, in the case of the recent border dispute between China and Vietnam, to each one of the three hundred thousand soldiers massed on either side. It's said that the effect of all these soldiers stopping what they were doing to tear open their envelopes and sit down to read a very long letter, bought the Chinese and Vietnamese leaders a valuable 55 minutes' time in which they could sort everything out over the phone.

Syvanos y Craxton has written splendidly on the nature of war and the necessities of peace. He once famously described war as 'a bother' and peace as 'a bluebird in flight but with rocks tied to its legs'. His dictums on the art of negotiation are legend.

'Talk down to the tall man, talk straight to the man of conventional height, and talk up to midgets.'

'Never trust a man who tucks his jumper into his trousers.'

'Always let your enemy think you are a fool, but quietly keep your mind sharp with crossword puzzles. Then, in the presence of your enemy, you can say: "Ha! You think I am the fool, but actually you are an even bigger fool, because I have confused you by concealing my intelligence. And therefore I have won the game of fools." This unfailingly produces developments.'

'Let your next move be unexpected. Over stalled negotiations, I once threw soup in Golda Meir's face, and she thanked me for it.'
[Syvanos y Craxton; *Collected Remarks* (ed. by Bono), Newfoundland Press, 1990]

Syvanos has written also the definitive account of the dark impulse which lies at the heart of human aggression:

Unhappiness cloaks our spirit like a sock. It ruptures the heart, as a pin would rupture a bee. Each man searches in vain for that still, silent moment of enlightenment, when confusion dissolves like sherbet and truth is loudly obvious. But that moment does not come. The sherbet stays dry and builds to a ball of anger so massive it rolls out of our hearts and onto our spleen. From there, it is but a short trip to the lungs, from which it easily rebounds on to the stomach. Inside each one of us is a sherbet anger-ball bouncing around at fifty miles per hour, and it only takes one act of insensitivity from a companion for us to cough it up and spit it in his face. I mean this figuratively.

[Syvanos y Craxton: *Hesitant Lemon Weaponry: Fifty-nine Figurative Explanations of Armed Conflict*; The Laughing Sailor, 1982]

Syvanos y Craxton's negotiating methods were always unorthodox but effective. Once, during talks about implementing a ceasefire among warring factions in Angola, Craxton recognized that the only way to get the twelve opposed delegations to agree was by optical illusion.

Instead of sitting everyone round one big table in the conference room, he set up three circular ones. The tables were all the same size, apart from the middle one, which contained chairs, pens, notepads and bottles of mineral water exactly 22% bigger than the other two. The effect of this was actually to make that table look the smaller of the three, since more of its surface area was dominated by stationery. Syvanos then told the delegates they could sit where they liked. Since none of them wanted to be near their opponents, they all rushed for the middle table, thinking that it was too small to fit everyone round it. The negotiations then proceeded for two weeks, with all twelve delegates sitting round the one table, and ignoring the two outer ones. The effect of this was to make everyone feel as if an agreement had been reached since no-one looked excluded, so they all signed a peace accord and went home.

It was only once the delegations got off the train and saw that all the fighting had stopped they realized how they'd been duped and were immediately beheaded by their army chiefs. War broke out again, but even here Craxton was able to impose a famous optical tranquillity. Rather than attempting to agree a ceasefire, he urged each faction on into battle, often spurring them with clumsy made-up taunts from their enemy camp. Craxton successfully calculated that if twelve military blocs fought against each other in a single precisely determined combination of alliances, and employing a carefully pre-established set of armed capabilities, the effect of this would be that the armies would cancel each other out and enough stalemates would be reached to make it look as if no war was actually happening. So, by goading each side on to just the right amount of violent attack, Craxton was able to implement what still looks like a lasting peace when viewed from a distance, though close up is in fact a total war that has so far cost a hundred and twelve thousand lives.

This is in keeping with Syvanos' most famous assertion that 'before one has peace, it is of course necessary to have a war on which to impose it'. It also explains why, as a youth, Syvanos was famous for assassinating prime ministers and blowing up swimming pools in high season, before giving all this up to receive his first peace prize in 1964. We wish him a happy birthday.

A LIFE AT THE OPERA

Opera is the coming together of music, theatre, design, people and coughing in the greatest synthesis of art capable of collapsing at the beep of a watch-alarm. It is man's highest creation, his most expensive assertion of artistic supremacy over the inferior beasts and birds of nature who, proficient though they might be with sticks and spittle, can't perform tricks as staggeringly complex as mounting a three-act declaration of love from a wooden castle. Foxes don't sing and leverets are incapable of costume design, so they needn't bother trying. Armies of termites, though they try impressing us with their twenty-foot high mud constructions, haven't a hope in hell of building anything out of wet dirt as architecturally elaborate as a publicly-funded opera house, with its dazzling honeycomb of boxes and its awesome web of sturdy crush bars. Have I made myself clear, animals? We're better than you, so go back to doing what you do best, which is sniffing at bushes.

This is what opera is. It's the rustle of programmes and clack of glass-cases of several thousand people anticipating grandeur. A few of those people are celebrating their birthday, many are romantically involved with others in the audience, some are dying, several are currently being burgled, one or two are planning to run away tomorrow, five have grit in their eye, one lost her dog to a temporarily out-of-control recovery vehicle that morning, more than you think are currently passing on an unpleasant dietary virus to their neighbour, over a third will find the whole evening didn't quite match their expectations.

The conductor. Was knighted five years ago for making terrifying demands on his horn section. Is a single man, dedicated to music and bitterness, secretly nurturing a reputation for shambolic jacket/trouser coordination to procure that title of 'genius' which the newspapers have so far forgotten to award him. Has the pervasive breath of claggy mint gums, which he regularly puffs across the violins and cellos, who call him 'Menthol Mickey' in tea-bar rehearsal breaks.

He comes on.

The audience now applaud the respect and admiration the orchestra fling at him in his pit. From this underground nerve-centre, he bobs his little white ground-levelled head round to smile at the line of eager and disappointingly-shod feet he's playing to in the front-row stalls. As the applause dies, he catches sight of a slightly furled sticking plaster jammed under old tights and badly masking a moon-shaped scab on a thick leg, and turns to start the music.

Music. Strange this, coming from under the stage and for the first ten minutes all we've got to look at is a heavy curtain with the crest of a crowned unicorn mounting a heron. But the first notes strike us as lovely and we start giving the experience the benefit of the doubt. Meanwhile, the burglars jemmy their way in through an upstairs window and start looking for the video. The rustling in the circle falls to a minimal patter as the music swells. People do hold their breath like they're meant to, though one individual is just frozen in the sudden realization she forgot to book a clown for tomorrow morning.

The Prelude to *Tristan and Isolde*. It lays before us the themes which will dominate the evening's performance. Wagner's peculiar chord near the start, pinpointing everything from Isolde's doomed love for Tristan to Tristan's extraordinary annoyance at having his emotions jerked around by somebody's love-soup, crowded onto a little blurt of sound which the programme-notes tell us turned the music-industry upside-down. For years after the first performance, people went around whistling the Tristan Chord, which they would normally have to do in groups of seven, or on their own if they happened to have a uniquely damaged mouth.

The music continues, and Menthol Mickey's arms form spindly shadows on the front curtain, attaching giant black rotating antlers onto the head of the raped heron. This is passionate music now, and the sound from the orchestra slushes and glides around in a slowly blossoming wallow. The audience make last-minute assessments of near neighbours, calculating from the frequency of coughs and the guessed texture of the liquid mix jumbling around inside whether the offenders are having a final clear-out or are digging themselves in for an evening's phlegmish sabotage. This uncertainty threads uneasiness through a few minds, one of which now fills with pleasing images of the gentleman two rows in front having his mouth stifled with a trumpet and a hammer.

The music reaches a peak of intensity symbolizing Tristan and Isolde being at it like knives, and three rows from the back, inside a small woman, on the upper row of her gums, four in from the left, a tooth begins to hurt. The tooth was attended to yesterday, and didn't like the experience and has now decided to give his owner a little nudging reminder of what he can do when he puts his mind to it. 'I dutifully masticate for you, my lady governess,' he professes, 'and I yield to your brushing and scraping without qualm or worry. I sit guard for you all night, and I endure deposits of nut and tomato skins with openness and true hospitality for these, my new visitors. And, lo, you reward me with drills, and my payment is needles. My heart is hollowed out, and filling composite occupies my soul. Is this, then, how my service is spurned, oh wicked lady? Am I an outcast on your gums? Then I shall make known to you the vent of my fury, by summoning the twang of my brother Root and sister Nerve. Feel you now the power of my anger? This is nought to the suffering I can assemble if you shame me with full purpose!' His owner makes a mental note to book a further appointment.

The music diminishes, and the curtain rises as the thieves find the video and start disconnecting the aerial. In a house four miles away, a professional clown who had been expecting a call that day sets off disappointedly for a walk in the night, realizing the tomorrow morning which he'd provisionally set aside for work will now be wasted. This is the fourth disappointment in as many weeks, and propels his mind closer to thoughts of retirement. The curtain carries on up to reveal the drift of the evening. The arrangement of shapes and colours on stage will determine whether the audience smiles at the welcome arrival of an old friend, or frowns in anticipation of an evening blighted by modernism, like a dinner spoiled by a daughter's art school boyfriend.

This evening falls somewhere in between. Familiar bits of building and rampart are hung in a peculiar combination (one man is upside down) but the settings are shatteringly far from the Cornwall of the original story (Act One takes place in a European sauna). It's apparent the audience will have to do some work for their average of £34.

And over there are the soloists, Isolde bound against her will for a forced marriage with an enemy despot while illicitly harbouring unrequited love for her father's killer, and her trusty maid telling her it could be worse. As they sing and towel themselves in the shadows and beautifully lit darknesses of a guarded steam room, it's clear this evening we're going to be in the company of an Isolde who is colossal.

Opera can be unkind to the massive. It thrives almost exclusively on prolonged demonstrations of love and captivating beauty, yet has constructed traditions of vocal power and range which demand these love anthems be projected from a big chest. Bulky singers have to fight against the obvious stupidity of the undertaking by producing sounds which transcend girth, and hoping to God the Director doesn't ask them to roll around on an upstage forest glade. This is the governing doctrine of our highest art.

Later, we find that Tristan too is colossal, so the love story does at least carry some conviction. Whether that's enough to conquer the mounting ludicrousness of the artistic proposition offered this evening will take at least another four hours to determine. Despite some knowledge of the music, despite even a familiarity with the peculiar habits of opera, there is still a detectable, sniffable gas of suspicion wafting across the audience that they have paid to watch a huge bad thing. Apart from the disgusting size of the participants, a hundred other points of absurdity produce dangerous sparks. That faint creak and wobble of the scenery, the thickening grills of sweat down Isolde's back whenever she sings near charcoal briquettes, the sometime written randomness of the melody, the moment when Isolde's maid snagged her scarf on a small handle jutting from a boat at the back of the stage made from fridges, those points of loudness and loftiness of pitch which unavoidably turn in to a pained shrill (two thousand knees are briefly tensed), that unfortunate play of light and shadows which at one point projects on to the back-cloth a silhouette of Tristan, short and stumpy save for a pitilessly elasticated stomach. The evening could go up in flames at any moment.

And yet the music just about banishes that threat. Out of passages only moderately captivating, come regular bursts of overwhelming glory that grab concentration, dim pulsing teeth, usher someone away from thoughts of baking, another from planning tomorrow's elopement, a third from still felt contempt for his doctor. As the sounds soar and mingle perfectly, the evening makes sense, the stupidity is forgotten and the burglars and the rain and the hundred cars outside and the fight forty yards across the street and the disgruntled clown and this morning's news about the Egyptian President and the pictures of his collapsed bike are now nowhere, and then someone sneezes, which is when, somewhere in the middle of Act Two, in a radical switch to the American mid-West, we return to a stage full of big people and papier-mâché cacti.

The evening tos-and-fros between these two states of appreciation. The music constructs an opera of ideal beauty and total tragic conviction, while our eyes apprehend something tiptoeing on the borderline with the abysmal. These two forms happily gallop in parallel, but occasionally merge in magic moments of believability, when for a brief second the only thing that seems real is an enormous couple singing German laments about fatality while wearing stetsons and rejoicing in love at a Kansas rodeo. Once the magic is dissipated, by the drop of a purse, or the demented half-time rush of the parched to the interval bar, like bison to a breeding ground, leaving Tristan behind, now kebabbed on someone's spear to start dying in German out of everyone's hearing, slowly fading while tethered to a still moving mechanical bucking bronco, it's easy once again to gaze at watches and flick through programmes, and to take in wider views not only of the stage but of the conductor's feverishly bouncing head demanding adoration from a bassoonist being slowly suffocated in a cloud of stale peppermint, and wider still to see the patchwork of cemented haircuts along the front rows and gaze up to the sides of the building, noticing the boxes from which people view events from a severe angle and to wonder what the Queen makes of all the performances she is forced to see bent round at seventy-nine degrees, and whether she remembers the evening not for what she saw on stage but who she was staring at across the theatre. What must life be like when viewed constantly from a right angle? Does the Queen grow up thinking that all playwrights stage dramatic action to take place out the corner of one eye? Does she have her favourite sides of actors? Does she consider Shakespeare to be our greatest slanty dramatist? Has her right ear grown to twice the size of the left one? Funny things ears. Two gnarled flaps of flesh hanging from the face, like skin from an old pair of cheeks retrieved from the waste-paper basket for alternative use. Starched face-flannels. The only parts of the body to look like Ireland. Which is better than looking like Egypt, which surprisingly is almost completely square. All that history and culture, stretching back a considerable number of millennia, squeezed into a country with straight sides. Why doesn't its borders bulge? Scotland's had less history but it's got burst edges like Kennedy's head in Dallas. And now Egypt's President has a punctured head too, and the whole world woke this morning to pictures of that flattened bike and wondered how such a freak accident could have occurred and why the keepers at the zoo had been so lax. God in Heaven, that music, though, familiar and twisted into cliché through over-use in romantic films and ironic underwear commercials, here suddenly seems shocking, heard for the first time, magnificent, as Tristan lies dead on a seventeen-foot-wide buttercup, and Isolde chats musically about love and dying and movingly sings 'oh dear', and it thrusts and soars up again, and sounds obviously obscene, and dies to a trickle and once again everyone has forgotten everything, but now the applause reinstates normality as the cast bows to Menthol Mickey, and someone hands a basket of flowers to Isolde, who looks not the slightest bit surprised, but would be, you think, if they handed her a basket of scampi or a live chicken, and already people are leaving, and the bitter tooth throws another tantrum, and the singers come on just one time too often, and the applause sounds shirty now as the theatre empties and the burglars accidentally tip over an ashtray which deposits stains on their shoes helping police establish their shoe-size leading to the arrest of one of them and his imprisonment for eighteen months in a cell half a mile away from this building where he listens to a recorded transmission of this evening's performance because he likes opera.

And that's what opera is, and this experience is exactly the same for millions of people all the world over.

DEFENDING THE RIGHT
TO CHOOSE (ALBUMS)

OK, here they are. The top one hundred albums of all time. You may not agree with the selection, but you must surely agree I am the only person who's entitled to make it. So, if you don't have these essential albums next to your midi system then you deserve no company and even less of a life. Got that?

1: Runrig: **Mara** (1992) The quintessential rock group, with the quintessential album of all time.

2: **Four Weddings and a Funeral: Original Soundtrack** (1994). The beat of a lost generation who suddenly found their way.

3: Fox: **Single Bed** (1973). Need I say more?

4: The Beatles: **Anglo-Irish Relations** (1965). Perhaps not as strong as **Revolver,** but how can we leave off our list the album that contains the superb **Gonna Eat You All The Way?**

5: The Travelling Wilburies: **Wilbury Salad** (1993). Classic album from this appalling group of individuals.

6: Top Of The Pops **29** (1978). The one with the girl in a purple top.

7: Robson & Jerome: **Achtung Baby** (1995). Their surprisingly successful U2 cover album. Magic.

8: Pan Pipes: **Tranquil Moods** (1992). The haunting sounds of the pan pipes played by The Peruvian Pipe Players. A revolution in your ear.

9: Joe Cocker: **The Theme from Thunderball** (1979). Little known, but essential. Joe Cocker sings the opening songs to all the Bond movies.

10: **Mask: The Movie Soundtrack** (1989). Uplifting music from the film (not the Jim Carey one, but the other one with Cher as the mother of a boy born with only half a face). Some solid dance tunes.

11: Brian Ferry and Roxy Music: **Again, Again, Agriculture** (1975). Thirteen moody tracks, thirteen controlled explosions within the city centre of contemporary culture.

12: **Senses: Twenty Contemporary Moods and Themes** (1994). An instrumental feast of familiar TV melodies. Mostly by Mark Knopfler.

13: Orchestral Manoeuvres In The Dark: **Starlight Express** (1988). Songs from the show, but slowed down a bit. Revelatory.

14: The Velvet Underground: **Guns** (1969). Shocking. A hundred and ten minutes of guns, all fired in one day.

15: Enya: **Feels Like Teen Spirit** (1993). Classic Gallic grunge.

16: REM: **Pardon My French** (1986). Unknown classic. Some of the tracks are surprisingly Cockney.

17: Pan Pipes: **Pet Shop Pipes** (1991). Pet Shop Boys' hits arranged for pan pipes. Almost uncontrollable.

18: The Who: **Götterdämmerung** (1978). Unbearable, but it works. This rock-opera is even better than Wagner's original. What's more, it *is* Wagner's original!

19: The Doors: **Summer Holiday** (1966). Astonishing.

20: Ron Wood: **I've Got My Own Album Now** (1979). Much better than anything the Rolling Stones ever did together.

21: The Edge: **The Edge Sings Cole Porter** (1992). And while we're on solo albums, how could we miss out this platinum collection of partly acceptable numbers from the leading U2 guitarist? He does a magnificent version of **The Lady Is A Tramp**.

22: Pan Pipes: **Pipal Scream** (1995). Pan pipes cover of both Primal Scream albums. There's no stopping them.

23: T Rex: **Sadly Fat** (1972). Notorious album cover of a pregnant chaffinch.

24: Haircut 100: **Nuns and Divorcees** (1984). Twelve songs about older celibate women. Curious.

25: Jimmy Hendrix: **All The Time In The World** (1968). The original to Louis Armstrong's bastardized Guinness classic.

26: Jim Carey: **Jim Carey Whistles Themes From Mask** (1994). An interesting experiment. Comic actor Jim Carey whistles film music taken not from his own film, **The Mask,** but from the earlier film, **Mask,** in which Cher plays the mother of a boy with a partial face. Both moving and hilarious. At the time, only twenty copies were sold.

27: Genesis: **I Can't Dance** (1994). Not very good.

28: Pan Pipes: **Pan Weller** (1996). Classic pan pipe arrangements of all the songs from Paul Weller's **Stanley Road. The Changingman** seems more written for pipes than it ever was.

29: **Truly, Madly, Deeply: The Complete Soundtrack** (1993). The entire movie, including all the dialogue, on a double album. That year's surprise club hit. Still popular in Europe.

30: Tony Benn: **The Benn Diaries** (1995). Includes **Jim Callaghan Took Me Aside,** and **Agenda For Jobs (Agenda For Growth).**

31: The Little Tiny Men: **The Little Tiny Album** (1965). The Sixties' godfathers of Britpop with their one glorious album. Includes **I'm In Love With The Little Tiny Sky.** Unfortunately, the group all died out within a year.

32: King Crimson: **The National Anthems of The World** (1970). Not their best. In fact, probably their worst, but quintessential none the less.

33: Scaffold: **Scaffold, Live At Central Park** (1978). A glorious memento of a strange day. A hundred thousand New Yorkers were unmoved by **Lily The Pink**.

34–92: Whigfield: **The Whigfield Anthology** (1996). One of the most ambitious projects in recording history. Fifty-eight albums of out-takes, demos, and tone signals from Whigfield's studio sessions. Of enormous relevance.

93: Pan Pipes: **Prince of Pipes** (1984). An early masterpiece. Peruvian pan pipes anticipate all of Prince's hits several years before they're released. Groundbreaking.

94: Abba: **Hump Me** (1976). A surprise.

95: Michael Jackson: **Parp!** (1988). Funk meets vintage cars.

96: The Sex Pistols: **Hello Dolly** (1979). Considered shocking at the time, now regarded as merely ridiculous.

97: **Indie-Pipes** (1996). It doesn't get any better than this.

98: Terence Trent D'Arby: **Grant Unto Us Our Daily Bread, Oh Lord, That We May Enter Into The Fullness Of Thy Wisdom As Ye Watch Over Me and My Girl** (1992). Quite good.

99: Bruce Hornsby: **House of Chickens** (1994). Why is this here?

100: Shaggy: **Boombastic** (1995). May one day be considered the best album of all time. Watch this space a hundred years from now.

RE-RELEASED SLEEVENOTES

The Album came out in October 1990, by which time we were ready to split, and many people thought it would be our last one, but in the end we did another eleven. Holly and Billie and Dave and the Atherton Twins left the band in the summer, leaving just me and Colin, our manager, but we decided to keep on pumpin' and kept the name. (Although Colin changed his own name to After Colin.)

Though all the others left, I don't think it's made much real difference in sound. Maybe it's a bit thinner but, y'know, that's how we were going anyway, since we hadn't used instruments on our last four albums. Certainly, the public thought we were still strong and bought the thing, for which I'm eternally grateful, and I keep on thanking them whenever I meet one of them.

This is the album I like best of all. That's not to say that everything we've done since hasn't been as good, so I wish you would just leave me alone and stop asking me those kinds of questions. Everywhere I go now, I get you guys from the media all shouting after me things like 'Why are your albums unfortunately not good any more?' and 'What happened to your albums? They're now appalling.' I mean, you've just got one story, haven't you, that the last ten albums are a mound of turkey-cack? You don't look at the thing positively, do you? You don't think: hey, maybe we was wrong. Maybe they're actually an improvement musically. Do you? No. So, until you do, I don't want to go down that avenue of talking about the possibility I've just been poohin' uniquely bad music out my ass for the last six years.

So, here's how we wrote and recorded the album. We'd been touring for seven or eight months, and one of our bassists said he was getting kinda homesick and killed himself. So we all thought it was time to get back home, but we were contractually obliged to carry on with the tour, so what we did was we all arranged for our homes to be shipped out, brick by brick, and taken on tour with us. So, then we thought, let's ship out the studio and our publicist's offices as well, and then maybe we can put some of this crazy stuff down on audio-tape and perhaps make a record, a sort of homage if you like, to our bassist but without having to incur financial penalties on cancelling the tour. So we did, and Geoff and Taylor and Graham-Mary all said what we had to do was make a real good album, an honest thing with measure and depth and plenty of chutzpah and zabaglione, so that's what we did.

The Tracks

1: I wanted to open the album with something honest and carefree, so I decided to write this song about the Vatican. I wanted to make it a love song, and Tommy, Keith, Bald Sam and Vincent gave me the idea of it being something sung by the Pope. I wrote it that night, sorted the riff out by 5am and had the thing in the shops by the opening of next day's trading. It's basically a bluesy number, but with the chords double-looped to give them that Street-Porter sound we were all in to then.

Papal Blues

My clergy's done left me
My bishops look confused
I've no sons and daughters
And I've got the Papal blues.

All alone in these apartments
Making edicts by the score,
When all I want is you babe
This Pope's sure feelin' sore.

You're the brightest babe in Rome, girl
And I've got the whitest smock.
I saw you from the balcony
As I stood to bless my flock.

But you turned and left me, honey
And went back to your hotel.
Now I'm scattrin' impure thoughts
Across my monastic cell.

The Papal blues done shake me,
Send a fever 'cross my brow,
'Cos if those bishops knew my sin
They'd start a holy row.

So, I'll shut Saint Peter's Church, girl.
My evening prayers I'll cancel.
Instead we'll dance in my basilica
And tango up the chancel.

I'll sit and make you flowers
Carved from candle wax
And thread you fine necklaces
From martyrs' bones in sacks.

We'll kiss through Armageddon,
And prance till th'end of time,
Choose Judgement Day to wed on,
And damnation for a fine.

> I'm celibate but I'm thru' with it
> I've got enormous Papal blues,
> So get your ass here quickly, girl
> And sit on my don'ts and do's.

(fade out to church bells and drums)

The song got protests from everyone, not just from the Churches but from the music industry as a whole. That's when this 'You really should give up' business started, and sometimes I would arrive back at my apartment and find that some nuns had got in and smeared things on my mirror like 'It's not the lyrics we object to, it's your singing, shit-mouth.' But I guess that's the establishment for you.

2: The next track, **Imagination Application**, is about the end of a relationship and the feelings that go through a guy's head when somethin' good ends with a woman, and you realize you've been so bad to her, and smacked her around, and consistently imprisoned her in the cells run by the unofficial militia you've hired to police your rock palace. The sort of thing that I guess has been going on between men and women since Adam and his skirt, but I felt pretty bad after the break up with Sanja and Ami and wrote this song about how I felt about never getting back together with them again.

Imagination Application

> I can imagine
> A man with a back made of pine,
> And a pensioner under three.
> I can visualize
> Crystal pies,
> With fillings made from glee.
> But I could never imagine

You'd have the time of day for me.

I can comprehend
A friend of a friend
Bringing his dead mother round for tea.
I can hypothesize
Doing some exercise
On a jogging machine built for a flea.
But I just cannot imagine
You'd ever get back with me.

Imagine
A barking circle,
A backwards nanny,
A stair that goes up itself,
A rubber computer,
Some laughing oil,
And a one-inch tomb for an elf.
Now try to imagine
Being in the same room as myself.

No, I can imagine
A shy boxer
Who wants to be alone in the ring.
I can conceive
That God would believe
Gravity is held up by string.
Yes I can imagine
A toad that speaks Russian
And a radiator shaped like Patti Hearst.
But I cannot imagine
You'd speak to me
Without pelting me first.

(repeat the first three verses four times, to fade)

3: Everyone said the album got much better after these first two tracks, and I was particularly pleased with the third number, **What On Earth** . . . , my big ecology song which I co-wrote with the man who owns Ecuador. We all broke off from the tour to fly out there to make the recording, which we did over two days in the international departures lounge of his house. The whole lot was then re-mixed in London and Chicago, using samples shipped over from the Third World.

What On Earth Are We Doing To Ourselves (And To Each Other)?

Think of the rainforests
Sitting all empty.
Think of the atmosphere
Soiled like a panty.
Think of the ozone
Torn to shreds.
And those baby seals
With their concussed heads.

A thousand species
Disappear.
Around about
Once a year.
A thousand more
Are very poorly.
Can't we stop it,
Surely?

Our ecosystem's falling down, falling down, falling down.
Our ecosystem's falling down, we're all crazy.
Let's do something about it.

If only we got our finger out
And stuck it in the ozone.
We'd stop our polar ice caps
Sloshing about unfrozen.
There is hope, there is a chance,
The earth can be better,
If we switched to something like
A catalytic converter.

A million lives
Are lost
Because man
Can't be tossed.
A million more
Can be secure
If we used
Organic manure.

Our ecosystem's falling down, falling down, falling down.
Our ecosystem's falling down, we're all crazy.
But we really can do something about it.

We kill cows and kudu
To feed our mammon,
And slay the meek and hairy
For a hunk of gammon.
Yet our population
Grows fifty times its size,
And will get worse unless
We compulsorily sterilize.

One billion people
From Mull to Mogadishu
Daily propagate

Enormous issue.
Another billion
Accidentally spawn,
By dry humping
Without their clothes on.

Our population's going up, going up, going up.
Our population's going up, it's so crazy.
We must enforce a programme of mandatory birth control on
a massive scale.

What on earth are we doing to ourselves?
And each other?
What on earth?
What? What? What? What? What?
What? What?
On a massive scale.

(fade out for thirty seconds and then back up for another hundred
and ten)

Some people didn't like the sentiments expressed in the song, although
it soon became clear that many more didn't like the singing expressed
in the song. I sacked my voice coach and flew over Walter Matthau's
for the rest of the album. He brought his family with him and let them
all run around the studio during takes, including his mother. The
session musicians stormed off and we were left to complete the album
with the family operating the mixing desk.

4: Still, I think these were actually the happiest times making this
album, and I wrote the song which I'm most proud of, **Strawberry Jam
Man**. A lot of people ask if it's a personal attack on our ex-drummer,
Solomon, for being named the third party in the divorce proceedings
I took in turn against each one of my four ex-wives. I like to think I'm

better than that. There is a lot of hate in this song, but it's directed against male promiscuity generally rather than against one particular individual with a beard and a body odour problem that doesn't seemed to have stopped him frigging his way around half the backing singers in the northern hemisphere. It also didn't stop him suing me, though.

The Strawberry Jam Man

Strawberry jam man,
You do what you can man,
Strawberry jam man,
Spreadin' yourself around.

Lookin' for a slice of the action,
You think you're the big attraction,
But you've really got a nerve,
Putting strawberries in preserve.

What I mean by this is
Your flaunted kisses
Are like strawberries,

While your casual dealings
With other people's feelings
Can be represented by jam.

(ie. you're frozen hearted.
Hence the cold set jam with which I started.)

So . . .
You're the strawberry jam man,
Because you think you can man,
You're dishing out affection
Like a reduced sugar confection.

I don't need to sing the whole story;
The image is fairly self-explanatory.
I'm equating the type of guy you am
With strawberry jam.

(the first verse is repeated again, confidently)

5: In September, I was forced to take three months off to recuperate after being stung by a bee. It was then I got to thinking about mortality. Y'know, it's amazing how little we are in the bigness of space and all that mighty upness of the sky, and our lives can go in any direction at any time but we're not aware of it, so we carry on being teachers or doctors or successful musicians who are genuinely getting consistently better with each album, without giving it a second thought. I wrote **The Extraordinary Accident Song** as a sort of way of trying to come to terms with these feelings but to a country and western tune. A lot of people said the song helped them through moments in their own lives when they began to think 'Who am I?' and 'Why am I being cheated on?'

The Extraordinary Accident Song

Woman walking down the sidewalk
Automobiles gleaming past,
Twenty-foot sharks
Consuming unleaded plankton.
She remotely tilts the head upon her
Turning the skull-ball skywards
As her feet jettison the kerb
And perpetrate a shambolic crossing of the road.

Just then
A hen
From a pen

Transported on a truck from Montana to Maine
Cannot remain
Still, and flaps in pain.

Extraordinary accident,
Waiting to happen.
If only they'd stopped her
In the delicatessen.

Badly nervous of the traffic,
The woman collides with her own suspicion
That uneasy collisions will occur.
She apprehends an oncoming moment
Of danger, as she catches the suffering
Of the bird on the cusp of her eye,
And flinches in lady empathy
At its more feathery qualms.

Which is when
The hen
Flaps again,
This time hurtling over the side of the recently re-fendered
    truck
Into muck
On the road, and is stuck.

Extraordinary accident,
Waiting to happen.
If only they'd stopped her
In the delicatessen.

Now the woman hesitates naturally
Obstructed by the grounded fowl,
And in that succulent moment dripping with female event
The truck swerves to miss her,

And hits a biker who rams a tree
Whose leaves blanket the bird, who terrorized lays
An egg on which she treads.

She trips
And slips
On her hips.
And swipes her stiletto-caked feet through the yolk and up
    into the air,

Where,
With her pair
Of heels, she kills two men.

Extraordinary accident,
Had to happen.
They should have stopped her
In the delicatessen.

La lala la la lala la la la la.
Ooh la la lala la.

The record charted very well in Holland and Angola, and I was
particularly proud that it was chosen as the official anthem for the
International Festival of Chess in Canada. A choir of six thousand
children sang it in front of the Queen, who cried twice.

6: Because of the song's success, I decided to do a quick follow-up in
a similar vein. I spent the next week working on the album's second
accident song, **Girlfriend In A Coma**, a homage to the title of the
Smiths' song with the same name.

Girlfriend In a Coma

Girlfriend in a coma
Looks like Hannah Mandlikova
Whenever she served
To stay in the match.

Oh yeah.

The song wasn't as successful, and the taunting started again soon after.

7: I spent six months trying to come up with a final song for the album. I originally wanted something bold and brassy, but then discovered Rod Stewart was banking on doing the same sort of thing to end his album, so I started looking for something small and brassy, but a few weeks later ditched the brassy entirely and threw all my energy into the small. I was getting nowhere, Colin decided to leave me, as did my voice coach's family, and I was really low. Then late one night I started playing a few notes at random on the piano, not really meaning to come up with a tune or anything, but Bill and Geoffrey and Philippa and Dave the Horse and Steve were all in the room and they said 'Hey, hang on a minute, play that tune again.' So I played it, and Philippa said 'That's my tune, you thieving bastard. It's off my solo album.' So, she left as well.

By then I was in despair, but Gerald Grundy showed me a letter. It had words and music for a song, written by an old woman who sent it in as a tribute to some of my earlier albums. We looked at the song, and it was so beautiful that I knew then and there I had come up with my final song for my album. It was called **Shoplifting Girl**.

Shoplifting Girl

Stay while I report you.
You can't evade this man.
'Cos, my love, I've caught you
Running off with ham.

Ooh, you're a shoplifting girl
And you're committing an offence
By shoplifting, girl
At a superstore's expense.
Yes, you, shoplifting girl
You think you're so smart
'Cos you, shoplifting girl
Have appropriated my heart.

I saw your furtive glances
And though my mind was smote,
You took some stupid chances
Hiding chops beneath your coat.

Ooh, you're a shoplifting girl
And my heart's in your pocket
Yes, you're my shoplifting girl
And I want you to drop it.
'Cos you, shoplifting girl
Perpetuate deceit
'Cos you, shoplifting girl
Have meat, but no receipt.

I asked for your name
Then melted, oh Melanie.
But I know your game:
You're committing a felony.

Giblets might look nice
To an inveterate thief
But you'll pay a heavy price
For stealing frozen beef.

Ooh, shoplifting girl, yeah.
Come quietly, this is the manager.
Ooh, shoplifting girl, yeah
It's gonna be alright
Just one or two questions . . .
Hand over the venison . . .

I was pleased, but when people started saying this was the worst song I'd ever recorded I had a major re-think and thought about quitting the band. But in the end I just told everyone the name and address of the old woman who sent it to me. I hope the bitch had a hard time, because she deserves to suffer.

But, that said, I think it's a fine album, and I hope you think so too, but save some of your positive comments for the albums that came after it, because I think they're all good as well.

THE QUEEN AND I

Nearly twenty years ago, the Sex Pistols released 'God Save The Queen' and caused outrage by depicting Her Majesty with a safety pin through her nose. No-one had ever made her head look like a nappy before. They then sang the song on a barge going down the Thames in front of the House of Commons, causing further outrage. The song itself dared to suggest the Monarch ran a fascist regime, an automatic cause of record-breaking outrage. It was then banned from Radio One and obviously sank without trace.

Now, two decades on, the chances are that if the Royal Family were to get in a barge and sail past a Sex Pistols reunion concert, the public would deem them by far the more outrageous group of the two. After all, it took four Sex Pistols and the awesome marketing skills of Malcolm McLaren to build up a reputation for colourful vomiting and peculiar bodily mutilation, behaviour which Diana perfected on her own. The Sex Pistols' historically worst excess was probably spitting in public. The Windsors and their entourage did far worse in the open, impersonating tampons over the phone, regularly copulating with marriage partners other than their official ones, ramming themselves against cupboards, having bits of their anatomy sucked by the bald and the unscrupulous, spawning children from the loins of third party Australians and, worse still, consistently betraying a terrible penchant for living most of their wedded lives in separate bedrooms (sometimes in separate castles) while claiming this therefore made them happily married like any other couple.

The Sex Pistols were untidy, but not fools. The Royal Family are spick and span, but very, very weird. They claim their first duty is to their country, but spend more time out of it than most. They declare total devotion to their children, but their idea of playing games with the kids is to put them in a Wendy House in October and pick them up twelve weeks later for the Christmas holidays. They profess a love of wildlife and the environment (most of which they happen to own) but seem to think that because it's just possible to kill with kindness, it's therefore also legit to kill with shotguns.

Weirder still, they instruct their sons and daughters to get divorced by means of a letter, even though they all seem to live in wings of each other's houses. They're the only people in the country who are genuinely interested in what the Lancashire Fusiliers are wearing. They play Real Tennis and Carriage Racing, two sports that no-one else on God's earth knows the rules to, which is why the Royal Family is so good at them. They do not, however, know how to walk without awkwardly fingering their cuffs or placing their hands behind their back or, in moments of real bother, giving their hands to their advisers to look after. They live a life of receiving gifts of flowers from little girls and gold-leafed camels from sultans. Emotionally, they've never at any time given their children anything other than an extended handshake. Their ideal birthday gift is a massive extended hand-shake from the rest of their family. They're suspicious of commoner in-laws for their ability to hug voluntarily. They don't understand hugging. The Queen once tried hugging patients in a hospital ward. Unfortunately, it was a Burns Unit.

In times of national crisis or tragedy, the Royal Family doesn't share grief through the expression of recognizable emotion. They express it through staring at flags and inspecting rubble. They show resolve in the firmer extension of their hand-shakes. They receive curtsies with undaunted determination. They do terrific one-minute silences. But their shoulders aren't considered the best public place to stain with tears.

When in a good mood, they walkabout. When glum, they process. When wanting to show-off, they take the controls of a helicopter. They are surrounded by the renovated and newly-completed. They live with the smell of spit-and-polish, and endure a gleaming life. One reason we don't see any black soldiers in the Queen's Household Guard is that they're all given a fresh coat of white paint every morning before she passes through.

But the interesting development lately has been that we're all beginning to realize how weird the Royal Family is. Weird not merely for what it represents as an institution, but for the type of individuals they actually are. They're harmless nutters, like that strange lot down the road who mostly keep themselves to themselves but breed polecats in the back garden and whose Dad always stands at the window in a string vest shouting to his kids to get down off the rusted Triumph Herald he's renovating on the front lawn, while his wife wanders about wearing just a purple shawl and some slippers.

It's like the scales have suddenly dropped from our eyes, and we can see what foreigners have always seen, that we live in a slightly weird country, but with a very, very weird family at its head. As the Windsors beckoned more and more documentary teams into their five-hundred-foot-long front living rooms, the gamble that this would endear them to the nation by making them look all the more ordinary backfired. We just saw in awesome detail how ridiculous a notion their collective lives had become.

The world is composed of many examples of the faintly ludicrous, but for the most part we turn a blind eye to the incongruities. Sport, the Vatican, a Geneva Convention on the recognized rules of war, hula hoops, ties, and the hats middle-aged ladies wear at weddings, are all faintly absurd concepts, but when viewed through squinted eyes just about get away with making some sort of sense. So we grant them the benefit of the doubt and decide just to get stuck in and enjoy them. This used to be what we did to the Windsors; we made them regal and then asked them to perform. But now, something indefinable has happened which has ruthlessly forced us to stare at them with wider and more unbelieving eyes. And deep down, I think more of us know that it now doesn't matter which way the succession passes. Whoever succeeds the Queen will have had a weird education, a weird voice, a weird marriage, weird hobbies and a weird walk. And more and more of us will find it deeply unlikely that we could ever curtsey or bow to him without quietly but continuously laughing in his face.

WHY YOU MUST FEELGOOD

It's official; politics is now a branch of metaphysics. The introduction of the Feelgood Factor into everyday political discussion has transformed the management of the British economy into a phenomenological debate about illusion and reality. Suddenly, what matters is not whether there is more money sloshing around our purses, but whether we *think* there is. Theses are now being written about individual perception and its relation to mortgage repayments. Somehow, the very act of imagining is seen as a sufficient means of transforming the climate of opinion and once that climate is transformed, argue those peculiar, forty-seven-year-old, sexless men we call Economists, then confidence will grow, investment will swell proudly, and we'll return to an economy that's both bulbous and cocky.

There's been a trend in recent years to talk of giving power back to the individual, so, I suppose, the Feelgood Factor is the ultimate weapon in the individual's armoury. It supplies each one of us with the power to by-pass reality and create a much prettier world in our imagination. The nagging claims of objective reality needn't now be addressed – the nation's rivers coagulating on discarded effluent and trout with ME, the sapped teachers and staff nurses spotted at night crying on the top decks of buses, the coiled cack that blotches our pavements, the long and honourable state tradition of sexually abusing the mentally handicapped in urine-soaked country houses, the startled four-year-olds ping-ponged between dumbstruck parents and professionals high on paperback theories about the wellbeing of children's bottoms, the police forces, frustrated with the criminal's inability to leave behind sufficient evidence, now openly calling for the manufacture of crimes to fit the punishment – all these things, what Britain today is like 'in real terms', can be chucked in favour of what we merely perceive to be real. The world can be whatever we want it to be, and if we can be persuaded to imagine it as a good world, then we might just reward those who allowed us to think that way.

We're now witnessing an increasingly popular form of statecraft known as virtual politics, where the daily agenda is driven by this quest to influence the imagination. Today, pollsters stop us in the streets and, like empty-faced Scientologists out on a recruitment drive, ask us if we feel happy. The fate of the nation hangs on the reply.

Since the onus is now on politicians to make us feel content, the search is on for happiness rather than an integrated transport policy or plans for the reorganization of local government. But what is happiness? As questions go it's a toughie, up there with the big metaphysical superstars like 'What is truth?' and 'Does human suffering have a half-life?' and if four thousand years' worth of human reflection hasn't been able to come up with an answer, the chances of people like Kenneth Clarke or Douglas Hogg succeeding must be slim. Of course, they don't have to tell us what happiness *is* exactly, they just have to make us feel it, but even Christ, who was more impressively qualified than Douglas Hogg, failed on this one.

Since feelgood politics is based on perception, it may be that politicians have to concentrate more exclusively on influencing the brain's ability to perceive. The distribution of strong hallucinogenics may help here, whether in powder or tablet form, as well as hypnosis. Optical illusions, from simple card tricks to the much more sophisticated publishing phenomenon of the *Magic Eye* books, are useful for momentarily confusing the senses' ability to recognize established patterns of reality, so it might be a good idea to publish economic data in this form, or underneath comforting pictures of cats playing with balls of wool. Uri Geller should be installed in the Home Office and a programme of mass lobotomization carried out in the South East.

This, of course, assumes that at the moment the British public don't feel good. I'm not sure this is the case. For, as I look around me, I see more and more faint traces of a smile on people's faces. The smile isn't one of financial security or social wellbeing, but is stimulated by a growing sense of certainty among us that very soon the whole damn load of clammy, innumerate, Europhobic, rate-capping, utility whoring, supergun smuggling, wayward penised carcasses who've been incompetently slabbering around the corridors of power for the last eighteen years will be really, actually and measurably out on their arses for ever. And, even if it turns out not to be objectively true, it still makes me feel good just to say it.

FACTS AND FANCIES

i) What happens when ideas die? After things like Existentialism and Perspective have run their course, do they go to an ideas heaven, where they can romp around with Aesthetics or Protestantism? And little ideas, what happens to them when they go too? Will there be tiny fossils of Marketing lying around in deserts forty thousand years from now? What does Jazz's skull look like?

These questions may be answered sooner than you think because we appear to be present at the Death of Ideas. (Death, of course, being one of the most popular ideas around, until most people abandoned it thirty years ago in favour of New Clothes.) This age is witness to what is known as the Dumbing Down of culture, a shrinking of perspectives and intellectual expectations which has seen more and more brains choose the easier mental options available when processing new ideas. So, the video of *Pride and Prejudice* is preferred to the book, while bowling is preferred to Seamus Heaney.

Above all, we're being warned of perceived trends in intellectual play away from reading and on to watching. We're told that books scare us, that Proust is a bucket of yawn, that Bertrand Russell couldn't fight his way out of a Boredom Tent, even if the flaps were open with a sign next to them saying 'This Way Out of The Boredom Tent, Mr Russell'. Books are dying, and the printed word is coughing its last inky phlegm in front of a berserk stampede to the electronic.

This last phenomenon takes the form of virtual reality games, CD-ROM frolics, Media Studies courses on triangular love-pulls in

Emmerdale, and the powerful new information tool of readily available porn on the Internet. The learned fans of densely-typed reading berate our rush to convert all knowledge and experience into entertainment packages, so that, for example, the sum total of man's inquiries into the spiritual and theistic impulses within human consciousness, something which it once took St Thomas Aquinas thirty years and forty volumes to capture in his *Summa Theologiae*, now appears as William Shatner's *Foundations Of Theology*, a CD-ROM package in which:

the highly-regarded Star Trek actor presents his own superbly illustrated guide to the world's systems of theology with an inimitable sense of fun. He illuminates everything from the Hindu theory of re-incarnation where 'rabbits can get their own back on dogs by returning as elephants, and where I'm sure even Mr Spock could find someone he'd rather be!' to a thrilling exploration of Methodism and what it feels like to be a Methodist, by playing an action-game in which chance has been eliminated and you are therefore technically not gambling.

[Sleevenote to William Shatner's *Foundations of Theology*, Soulmaster,

CD PC £39.99]

The fear is that, shying away from complexity and seriousness, our brains will gradually diminish and selected head-muscles rot. Sated on the conga but starved of Kafka, parts of us may shut down forever, unable to be re-opened for generations, like decommissioned collieries. The demand for visual stimulation is obliging more of us to communicate exclusively through arresting images so that, for example, teachers at school have to become more melodramatic when taking French lessons, and suicide notes now have to be more colourfully packaged. In an increasingly cretinous society the most basic of concepts have to be explained and simplified; 'Morality' becomes 'Not hitting', 'Truth' becomes 'Some things that are what they say they are, like in documentaries.' Our attention span becomes shorter and shorter and our attention span becomes shorter. We invent simpler religions with no commandments. An International Mathematics Convention lowers all common denominators. The world dumbs down into a universal *reductio ad absurdum* which nobody recognizes because we've all forgotten our Latin.

This is not unnecessary alarmism. Linguists have already noted that the number of surviving languages in the planet is diminishing, a revolutionary and frightening development. Species may die, the world may run out of marmosets and buttercups, but surely man wouldn't be stupid enough to mislay all his words? Masters of the imagination like H. G. Wells and Patrick Moore have created worlds where planets sing and time splits into shapes; none of them came up with a society where the adjective 'slabbery' simply didn't exist, or where most races forgot how to pronounce 'sultana'.

Words decay through lack of use – when was the last time you said 'behove' when ordering a pizza? – but so too might other parts of our social baggage. If we don't now exercise all our available emotions, is there not a possibility that some time in the future they too might petrify? Perhaps a hundred years from now, man will no longer be able to feel disdain, or be sarcastic. Internalized hostility may be wiped out from mainland Europe, while only a few inhabitants of the Caymen Islands will be capable of being impertinent. The world will become mono-reactive.

If words, the protective fur of ideas, are withering, then thoughts stand an even smaller chance of survival now they're being left for naked.

ii) That's what some people are worried about, at any rate.

Others dismiss this view as the sad ravings of someone who's just spent a lot of cash on computer software but can't get the damn stuff to work. These riposters in turn herald the dawn of a new intellectual order, where the pc screen democratizes knowledge and the language of programming actually nudges thought into a new and infinitely productive three-dimensional pattern of creativity. Once children were forced to wrestle left to right with the piano keyboard, now they willingly accept the much more demanding co-ordinational challenges of trying to save your crew of three-necked Mandrioths from the advancing fire-cows of the enemy with only mag-blasters and sizzle-guns at your disposal. Working on seventeen levels, keeping four different games in play, and switching between six potential rates of difficulty has given the software-hardened child a much more dexter-ous and contrapuntal facility with spatial logic. Minds are now happy thinking three-dimensionally, darting from half-finished diversions to the start of fresh arguments and back again, like overjoyed monkeys in a cage-full of nuts. Could it be that as computers become the new paper, our speech starts to ape the distinctive patterns of pc communication? So that we can

separate off in our conversations partially completed utterances, to which we can return at a moments'

concurrently start new sentences, happy they too can be left dangling unfinished at the back of the mouth until further

notice, when we choose to connect them together in a carefully grafted utterance? Imagine how conversation would change in this new cut-and-paste order of experience. When we meet someone for the first time we may both decide to skip forward to the end of our dialogue and sort that bit of chat out first, then go back to the beginning now knowing how well things will go, and build towards the agreed conclusion via the rest of the exchange. Maybe a thousand years from now this non-linear processing of sensations will work its way into our biological make-up and we'll give birth to a generation that's born middle-aged and then works its way out at both ends.

It could be then that we're currently taking a cognitive leap towards a

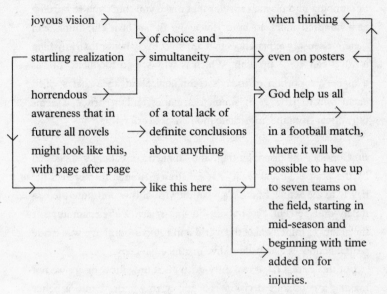

joyous vision → ⌐ when thinking ←
⌐→ of choice and ——
startling realization ⌐→ simultaneity——→ even on posters ←

horrendous → → God help us all
awareness that in   of a total lack of
future all novels   → definite conclusions   in a football match,
might look like this,   about anything   where it will be
with page after page   possible to have up
→ like this here →   to seven teams on
        the field, starting in
        mid-season and
        beginning with time
      → added on for
        injuries.

It's a chaotic prospect. But though this dive into micro-chip logic may rejuvenate the workings of the brain, there's still little evidence to suggest we might use it other than to play beat-'em-up games. For all the proclaimed advantages of the latest technology as a useful education tool, what shifts units in the shops is how good the graphics are when someone gets his stomach violently ripped from the inside of his back. Unless geography lessons can be illustrated with 3D maps of Istanbul being swallowed by Neptunian Plasma-beetles, people are just going to grow up gradually losing their sense of direction in the real world.

What they will have though, is a heightened sense of direction in an imaginary one. For many, the joys of simulation open up a branch of experience that seems much more fun, addictive, and maybe even safer than anything the dull here-and-now can suggest. Using smoke and music to wander round with harmless lasar guns in futuristic ante-chambers peopled by cardboard cut-outs of Sigourney Weaver, or climbing into plastic capsules that make you think you're hurtling at a hundred miles an hour down the throat of a chipmunk, can generate sensory experiences that are objectively better than anything a novel can come up with. Which is why we go for them. But as a higher proportion of today's technological advances get applied exclusively to parks, rides, simulators, games, and the virtual, it seems our retreat from the immediate moment is accelerating.

iii) Consider the disappointing, anti-climactic possibilities suggested by the phrase 'virtual reality'. It's a strange animal that prefers the nearly to the actual, but that's what the virtual is: a not-quite-there, a ninety-nine percent, a just-about-but-not-really. We're enamoured of the ability to impersonate the world and romp around in a well made partial fiction. We all want to live in a nice big copy.

But this retreat from real nitty-gritty; is it unwitting, or are we not making a conscious decision collectively to withdraw into a better world of fun? Do we not spurn intellectual possibilities by choice in favour of the obvious benefits of having a great time? Might we not be getting dumber deliberately?

I only suggest this because, for all the benefits to the information explosion which digital technology now presents us, it seems information is precisely the one thing more and more of us feel we've had enough of. The Internet gives us immediate access to everything from the dental records of all infertile hosiers in Marseille to the reading list of every university metallurgy faculty in Glenda Jackson's parliamentary constituency. It's clearly becoming impossible to function as a human being unless one can utilize such information.

Too much knowledge can also be a dangerous thing. As the wisest of us make fresh inroads into our understanding of matter stability and gene replication, it's only inevitable that the products of these discoveries will be a sequence of ominous bangs and freaks. Our quest to acquire comprehension of the world happens just a few seconds ahead of our slightly excited realization we can flatten it. Maybe Internet users have a point logging on in droves to **Lucy Lay's Gallery of Ass** rather than **Here's All The Information You Need On How To Make A Nuclear Bomb**. Species like the human race have marvellous defence systems, and maybe the one it's using now is its Stupidity Gene. Aware that too much information may literally be the death of us, we've started retreating from knowledge in a big way, spurning learning in favour of simulated water-slides and digital erotica. But while this protective ignorance is going on, ideas are dying, possibly at the rate of a good one every day.

There is, however, a way out of this depressing state of affairs; a solution which preserves our chances of survival by steering us clear of the Information rapids, but still keeps the brain ticking over on what used to be the different categories of knowledge before knowledge fell out of fashion. With one difference, though. The solution relies on Information-less Knowledge. Data of absolutely no value whatsoever, but following the established rules of learning. It's calorie-free wisdom. Dummy thoughts. Lobotomized facts.

For instance, wouldn't it be good to preserve the notion of Physics, even though we now regard physics as the one thing most likely to cause our skin to drop off? Why dissect the atom when you know it'll blow half your face to China? So, instead, why not devise a Stupid Physics, an entire system of study which can still exercise the mind but which follows useless laws we've just made up? A gormless system where nuclear particles bang into one another through sheer clumsiness and water forgets which temperature to boil at, or utilizing an oafish technology where we spend millions launching imbecile satellites that don't know where they're going or what to do once they get there. Consider the possibilities now at our mind's doorstep. Why don't we come up with a gaseous form of chicken? A new type of car that cuts down travel time by sucking its destination towards it? A bionic moth?

If digital technology is so good, let's try passing things like laundry and squirrels down telephone lines.

We can liberate our heads from the restrictive helmet of the actual, and instead have a great time childishly skateboarding around previously suspect halls of learning. What I'm proposing is a Manifesto of the Stupid, in which I urge society to embrace all advances in science, philosophy and literature, but get them wrong. Take your children out of school if necessary and at home teach them the benefits of not paying attention. Be bold enough to stretch their brains and let their cognition develop biceps, but by means of the ridiculous. Spend time with them on empty mental exercises like attempting to define the opposite of 'placard' or quantifying the difference between 'insight' and 'peeping'. In mathematics, introduce your offspring to the idea of bent fractions. In politics show them new theories, revolutionary in proposing an athletics stadium just for kings, and the government of the people by a team of sport despots. Encourage them to think about radical new fields of psychology, signalling advances in the practical ability of the mind to make jig-saw versions of its dreams and then sell them to toy-shops. Get them to write down a theology of daisies. Show them the sight in Palestine where archaeologists discovered the Wrong Gospel. Plan practical advances in agriculture and dairy farming begetting powerful challenges to environmental collapse with the invention of bonsai rainforests, only four metres in diameter, and semi-skimmed cows, three-quarters the size of normal cows and slightly transparent. Devise a new poetry, in which all words rhyme only with the name of the person who wrote them.

Above all, when confronted by the demands of the young inquisitive, lie. And raise your lies to an art form. Say that pollution is buried in the sky and that water is dug up from clouds. Tell them snails wander round with their houses on their backs but that some landlord snails carry pubs. Explain that the universe is gradually expanding because teams of architects are running out of control with God's money.

Show them the blue bits on old cheddar and tell them it's the mess left behind by cheese-lice whenever they have a barbecue. After all, don't we already feed our young on a diet of fibs about Santa Claus and dragons? Indeed, aren't novels, pictures, films and entertainment all massive lies? If we're to bring the next generation up ready for the virtual adulthood we're preparing for them, then let's do it with an absurd amount of vim.

Two-thirds of our lives have always been lived in a fabricated world – the abundant imagination of childhood and the mix of obstinate memories and confused perceptions that signal old age – so why not complete the loop by making adulthood daft too? We spend our responsible years driven by the abstract ghosts of fears and ambitions, so let's formalize this relationship with the non-real by setting up a University of Baloney from which we can graduate as the perfect completion of our education.

I've therefore advanced a Manifesto of the Stupid in the hope that in such a collusion between the peculiar and the dumb we stand our best chance of preserving what we truly are, minds in motion turning world to entertainment.

THE WORLD'S NARROWEST WAR

I once joined a queue outside a small shop advertising a sale of exciting goods at low prices. I came prepared with some provisions and a piece of yellow bedding. Two hours later, the number of people behind me had grown to maybe six or seven, but word soon spread that this was the queue to join and within a week we numbered fourteen thousand. The shop was still closed, however, and none of the shop officials who came and went could give us any firm indication as to when the exciting goods would become publicly available.

We dug in for a long wait. It was interesting to observe how different language communities tended to queue together (I was positioned in front of a long line of French couples and about three hundred yards ahead of a raucous kink of Spaniards). A system of communications soon developed so that it was possible to find out what was going on in all parts of the queue. Someone was having a wedding anniversary fifteen hundred yards away and we all clubbed together with the intention of buying her a brooch when we got in. The nights were balmy, and dinner parties and spontaneous pavement cafés grew up along the line. Systems of bartering and exchange evolved, and we made a simple currency out of our discarded jackets.

On the twentieth day, word came that other queues were forming across the Channel and were on the move. We had no idea whether they were hostile and so sent scouts out to film them (on primitive, improvised cameras which used a polyester film). A year later the scouts came back with evidence these queues had originally been attached to High Street sales all across Northern Europe but had then broken loose from their doorways. Once unfastened from these root shops they simply drifted free and started hungrily looking for discounts elsewhere.

What we didn't know then was that these queues had themselves launched a series of small probes up into the clouds. The probes spotted our queue, and the continental lines all linked up and headed our way. (Although some of them were fooled by other satellite evidence, and went off to attach themselves to the end of what turned out to be the Great Wall of China.)

We were still none the wiser about this gargantuan column's intentions, though. Would it join on to our end, or try to dislodge us from the front? We prepared for an onslaught.

Another year later, still with no sign of a start-date for the sale, we spotted the European queue on the horizon. It looked like nothing was going to stop its insatiable hunger for bargains as it swept forward. Little lines of people in its way were easily consumed by this powerful mass of waiting humanity. Within hours, the enemy queue was at our tail, just four or five feet off, where it then suddenly stood and kept an eerie silence.

They had not connected. They stood there, this multitude of some three hundred thousand souls, lying in attention mere paces behind us. And we, who had grown over the years into a considerable file ourselves, maybe numbering a quarter of a million patient individuals, could only wait in front of a door to Fenwicks and fear the worst.

Little did we realize what the worst would be. On the morning of the thousand and first day of our queueing, at precisely 11.30 am Eastern Queue Time, what we took to be an emissary from the enemy line walked across the no-man's-pavement separating our two big arrangements. She walked carefully towards us but instead of stopping behind the gentleman at the end of us, moved forward to some children four or five ahead of him and started barging in. Obviously everyone around tried repulsing her, but the damage was done. With our attention diverted it was an easy matter for another invader to move forward and shove in further up. Soon, the advance assumed a weary pattern as every thirty seconds another one came casually up and just pushed in as if they had every right to be there. On and on they came, one at a time right through the night, as rude as can be, until all three hundred thousand of them had perpetrated the largest incidence of mass skipping ever to have occurred in the northern hemisphere.

By the end, many of us had become demoralized and went home, but others stayed on to fight. Unable to dislodge most of them, we took their names and warned them we were going to report them to the manager of the shop once the doors were open.

And now we live with them in an uneasy peace. They outnumber us, and have started influencing our decisions with their insidious casual chat. They tell us that the stuff on the first two floors is worth avoiding, and that the real bargains are to be had up in the Bedding section on Floor Four. They suggest that shorter skirts and lighter trousers are probably not going to be the fashion this summer and that maybe we'd be better holding off for our clothes until next year's January sales. Some even claim they're not interested in the sale at all and have just come to return stuff. Many of us have become dejected and frightened. Meanwhile, the enemy queue-people keep letting their friends in.

No news has reached me from the door. I can only hope that the sales staff has spotted what's going on and have resolved not to let these monsters in. If so, then I will quite happily stand here for another three years until I see every last one of them drop. Our country's integrity over this position must be maintained, and their crimes must be avenged. I will defend my God-given right to buy a cheaper sweater even if it's the last thing I do.

A WORKABLE ALTERNATIVE
TO TRAMPS

Approaching an election, the politician's agenda naturally turns to thoughts of a higher moral order. In recent years, this has been most dramatically demonstrated by the urgent desire of all political parties to address the pressing popular issue of tramps and beggars on the streets and how best to charitably get rid of these good-for-nothing louts. Fortunately, Labour and Conservative now out-do each other in their moral revulsion at the sight of these messy wasters, and are happy to consider views which a year ago would have been regarded as repugnant and expensive. So, as our streets and public walkways become gridlocked with hobos, and it's impossible to go for a jog without treading on a wino's mouth, perhaps the time has come to harry the issue a little further with an intelligent scheme of my own, namely that everyone of no fixed abode currently slouching around our shoe-shop doorways or begging direct debits off innocent passers-by should be rounded up immediately, deloused and placed in central reservation points, where they can be instructed, numbered, and sold, as slaves.

Now, I understand this plan may prompt a few dismal ethical queries, but these are easily pricked by the superior claims of logic, which can readily demonstrate a natural justice in selecting for the vagabond and sozzled mendicant the function of slave. For this purpose, I draw upon the most respected system of natural order and civil conduct that we have today, namely the principles of sound economy. Let me explain.

Society is purely the balance of two opposing economic forces, that of supply and that of demand. Man is a working unit capable of supplying a utility (his own labour) in return for a demanded premium (his wages). However, by seeking money for nothing the beggar applies only one half of this monetary equation: he demands but he does not supply. This financial imbalance must be redressed if we're to prevent our entire economy collapsing for the sake of a few pennies given to a hungry mechanic from Doncaster, and the surest method of doing so is by implementing an equal but opposite system in which labour is provided but for which reward is withheld, ie slavery.

The re-introduction of slavery to these islands has much to recommend it. Our streets are littered with a large community of fit but currently functionless people who could provide useful and free skills around the house or workplace. Every household could take possession of a slave who, hardened to an outdoor existence, wouldn't require much in the way of accommodation to keep him happy. A young, keen and grasping beggar could be set to the fields, where his sharp appetite would drive him to forage for fruit and help pick sweetcorn harvests for farmers. A nimble runaway, no more than thirteen or fourteen years old, would make an ideal domestic slave, perfectly suited and shaped for household chores and capable of entertaining one's own children at very little extra outlay from the parents, perhaps even fulfilling the function of house-pet. A strong schizophrenic, not aptly suited for mental labour, could be given manual tasks that wouldn't tax his brain but to which his physical energies could be put (though those of the paranoid kind can, I'm told, make excellent alarm systems). Whores could do the shopping.

Add to their company other undesirable interferers in our freedom to walk around, such as the squeegy merchant, the bicycle courier, the rollerblader, the collector of public opinion, the seller of magazines written by the unhoused, the representatives of religion offering free personality tests, and the distributor of cut-price Tuesday-night invitations to city night-clubs, and we would have a mighty workforce indeed oiling the cogs of our society for an estimated expenditure of absolute zero. Not only that, but we would have the most glorious and uncluttered pavements anywhere in Western civilization.

I think a lot of people forget what it means to be able to walk the streets without fear of being asked to hand over tenpence. It's a God-given right. St Augustine in his religious classic *The City of God* describes a vision of a shining city of transcendent beauty in which immortal citizens (us) proclaim unending devotion to the Mystic King (God) for cleansing their marble boulevards of unpleasant looking minstrels. John Bunyan saves his sharpest words in *The Pilgrim's Progress* for the description of 'the sixteen Tramps of Reeking-Slovenliness' that sit at the gates of Vanity Fair, while John Milton's Satan in *Paradise Lost*

Stood blocking th'open portals of might Heaven
His arm outreached for pennies, mammon's pips,
And assaulted each unsullied entrant's nose
With sherry breath and undercoat enpissed.

Clean streets are part of Britain's heritage. The beauty of an avenue uncluttered by annoying men has often been regarded as the perfect outward symbol of a pure inner civic morality. That's why it's totally good that this righteous issue has at last moved to the heart of British political debate. That's why I too carry no shame in proposing my own plans for the entrapment and enslavement of this morass, since I have a deeper, more spiritual end in sight.

I carry a vision of golden streets, a network of clear and clean underpasses, where the civilian can do his or her business uninterrupted by distress. We must build a brighter Britain – if need be, an emptier Britain – in which all our children have access to a web of tramp-less superhighways reserved only for the purposeful. By ridding our roads of undesirables, we will be allowing the nation to go unhindered towards its destiny. We will be giving the people back their freedom to walk into a bakery, to stride across a car-park, to enter a tunnel. With freedom comes enterprise and commerce, and better bakeries, car-parks and tunnels will spring up along our streets because of it. Our roads will resemble a gleaming new metropolis of optimism, its boulevards made from rare metals and regularly winning design awards.

And we will all be happy. And we will walk home to our slaves at night and we will fear no evil.

ARMANDO IANNUCCI CAN'T COME
TO THE BOOK RIGHT NOW

Hello. I'm Phil, Armando Iannucci's next door neighbour. Armando's away on holiday at the moment and he's asked me to look after this bit of his book while he's gone. I know he was a bit worried that someone might break into it; he says these days you can only be gone for a weekend and before you know it Martin Amis creeps in looking for something to do. Once he starts chucking a few words together, apparently, he's 'harder to dislodge than a barnacle on heat' (Armando's phrase, not mine – I've never heard of him).

Anyway, Armando's given me a list of topics to discuss to make it look as if he's still here. Normally I'm a painter and decorator by trade, so I'm not usually called upon to take a wry glance at the world we live in, but then Armando and Auberon Waugh helped me out last week on a big decorating job over at Harlow so anything to return a favour.

First off, plutonium. I've been asked to say something about there being a lot of it around on the Black Market, now that nuclear reactors are shutting down faster than some of the old timber yards and Russian scientists are looking for a bit of cash in hand until better work comes along in the summer. And I must admit, for a scarce and dangerous substance, plutonium nowadays seems to be turning up as often as solid hardwood strip overlay patterns on kitchen floors (my phrase, not Armando's). Yet the Nuclear Inspection people are still having problems tracking down who's responsible for smuggling all the plutonium out of Russia.

As a painter and decorator I know what it's like trying to get hold of materials that are in short supply. You wouldn't believe the trouble I had to go to recently to get a particular type of mauve vinyl-laminated wallpaper border that would adhere to a rather over-crenellated wall and ceiling surface. (That's a whole chapter in itself: basically I had to get a special jar of P V A proprietary stripping compound sent over from a supplier in Ludlow.)

Anyway, what I'm saying is that we decorators are a rather resourceful breed of domestic maintenance specialists and it wouldn't surprise me if some enterprising Russian decorators were behind the location and shipment of plutonium within the international black market. It's certainly worth looking into.

The next topic that caught my eye was Bosnia. This operation was initially planned as a quick in-and-out job by N A T O, though the concern now is that the West will get bogged down in an intractable and complex political situation demanding much ad hoc military planning. In many ways, it's a bit like trying to apply masonry paint to an exterior surface: at the outset, it looks fairly straightforward, but, unless you prepare sufficient scaffolding, bring a long-pile roller for rough brickwork, and check the weather forecasts for any potential cold or frost (which can badly affect the water content of the paint), you're going to end up with a poorly coated surface. Perhaps Carl Bildt and his international friends should have sought the advice of a professional decorator before they went storming in without the correct preparation. I certainly think so.

Next, the OJ Simpson phenomenon. Much has been made of how the American media turned Simpson into a celebrity while forgetting the victims of this tragic domestic double killing. I for one would urge us to turn our thoughts away from the accused and onto others more deserving of our sympathy, not least of which is the decorator called in to clean up the house afterwards. I know for a fact he had to use a hardwood buffer at an industrial hire rate to get rid of some of the floor stains, and a steam stripper with F2 glasspaper to dry abrade some of the more awkward corners where stuff had caked in. So we should spare a thought for him.

And finally, Tony Blair. He's ditched the old Labour tax-and-spend policies, but hasn't proposed any detailed alternative. He says he doesn't want to paint himself into a corner before the next election, but I say that being painted into a corner is nothing to get frightened of these days; most emulsion paints dry within twenty minutes, and any scuffs or marks caused by stepping onto the painted surface Tony Blair could easily touch up using a small 12mm pure bristle brush, in my view the most suitable hand brush for accurate painting in small areas. So what are you running away from, Mr Blair? Paint?

And that's it. I'm off now to do a quick job for Germaine Greer, a ten-by-four close-type chapter in her new book on gender mainten-ance. Fifty quid for the whole job, and you can't say fairer than that. Not at today's prices.

A LIFE IN PICTURES

Death is a fickle hen, and random are her eggs. One dropped recently on Harold Wilson, the first Prime Minister I can ever remember. Some people mark their childhood with memories of thrilling football matches or crushes on the girl across the flyover. For some perverse reason, I seem to be able to phase my years up to and including adolescence in terms of Conservative and Labour administrations. That's why it was such an emotional wrench for me recently to hear of Wilson's demise: my first Prime Minister had just died. Unfortunately, I can't wander down to the pet shop and buy another one.

Let me be the last to offer a reassessment of the career of Harold Wilson. It can't be as comprehensive and fulsome as some of the more distinguished offerings from the likes of Hugo Young and Mike Yarwood, but I hope it offers the occasional challenging insight. Also, it's all true.

Harold Wilson appeared off and on in news programmes from when I was seven or eight, and then more regularly from when I was eleven. He had a pipe and a funny voice, and I impersonated him at school. I still have a prop pipe from that time. A couple of years later, he disappeared for a bit. Looking back, I now realize this was at the end of his first major period of public life, though he was to make a spirited comeback not long afterwards, embarking in the second Wilson era on a series of documentaries for ITV about former Prime Ministers, a BBC2 chat show he hosted called 'Friday Night ... Saturday

Morning' and, perhaps his boldest achievement, a guest appearance on the Morecambe and Wise Show.

I then didn't see him again until 1984 when, as a student, I attended a talk he gave at my university Economics Society. He seemed frailer then, and his speech became distracted. He told a long but amusing anecdote and then, half an hour later, told it again. He was the first really famous person I ever saw in the flesh, but the experience was an extremely sad one.

I've met other famous people since then (for example, Jack Dee) but this first encounter with what up until then had been an amalgam of two-dimensional memories inspired by newspapers and television was the most revelatory. When legend becomes flesh one appreciates how much the legend relies on a conspiracy of communicators to preserve its wholly independent existence. Journalists, broadcasters and now historians will guard and co-ordinate Wilson's life, enhancing or denigrating his reputation according to whichever political analysis of contemporary events happens to be in fashion. It's as if someone's entire past is handed over to the National Archive at the moment of death so that, as the flesh decays, patterns of life can be made and remade out of the transcripts and footage which remains.

Nowadays, brilliant technology means that the instant a death is announced, a fully-formed assessment of the life can be broadcast within seconds. Such is the media's determination to reduce to the merest slither the reaction time involved in this process, that we're now beginning to sense the first sniffs of a creeping media phenomenon, that of the present tense obituary.

It used to be that when men and women of greatness died it was only after a suitable period of mourning that everyone would lay into them. It was part of the traditional pattern of obsequies to lower the body into the grave and give at least two minutes' silence before running home to publish an account of the deceased's lurid private life. So, years elapsed before we learnt that W. B. Yeats stole all his poems off a small child. Or that Abraham Lincoln was secretly married to some caribou. Or that Gandhi got aroused when watched by Geordies. Nowadays, though, kiss and tell mourners sell their serial rights before the subject's mortal coil is slightly rusty let alone shuffled off.

But the dying are catching up. France's former President Mitterrand spent most of his dying breaths 'putting the record straight' on his long past and tiny future. The voluntary fine-tuning of one's life story betrays a fear of the ravages done to reputation after the brain and body close for business. Richard Nixon, apparently doomed by history's judgement to be seen as a massive Presidential arse-up, did his best to rewrite his life by spending retirement scuttling round China on worthwhile diplomatic missions. The effort may have paid off. At his eventual funeral the dead criminal was eulogized, if not to high heaven, then at least to a moderately attainable purgatory. Jimmy Carter is now attempting the same thing, salvaging a reputation by intervening in the disputes in Haiti, Korea, and, for all I know, the one between the dog and the cat kingdom.

Famous people are getting wise to the fact that a life lived in public becomes a story, not much different to us than *Citizen Kane* or *When The Boat Comes In*. They inhabit a sort of fictional life they've been partly responsible for creating, but unfortunately for them fiction must have an ending as well as a beginning and a middle. But think how attractive certain endings can be. For example, a hole in the head transformed the Kennedy Presidency, turning JFK from a friend of Marilyn Munroe who nearly blew up the world, into the first martyr in the chapel of liberalism. Gunning Kennedy down in public a year before elections seemed a neat way of bringing focus to an otherwise confused administration.

Professional cynics and fanzine editors have been quick to point out what a splendid idea it was for River Phoenix to die, cleverly by-passing the hard slog of David Lynch movies and Martin Amis interviews that would otherwise have been de rigueur for achieving cult status. It was a shrewd move, though it would have been better for all of us if it had happened to Keanu Reeves. There's something about a life lived on the public stage that demands an early death. To live beyond the most representative age of one's carefully cultivated image is unseemly. James Dean and Marlon Brando were the popular men's men of the Fifties. One died and stayed that way, the other lived on and rammed butter up an actress and wore leotards on the Planet Krypton.

The latter is now a member of the living dead; durable individuals victimized by our impatience with things that go on too long. The need for quicker and constant turnover of stimuli forces us to demand a more compressed life from everyone around us. Those who prefer to stick to a comparatively languid life cycle are dropped massive hints that their existence is no longer required. For famous people, the hints come in the form of a six-hundred-page biography and a vandalized statue in a park; for the less well known the clue is a room in an old folk's home with a five-year diary by the dresser. No wonder the Pope looks so aggrieved these days. He does his leg in and immediately his Private Secretary throws some wax on his face in an attempt to get a death mask into the St John Lateran's Gift Stall by noon.

The more we grow up in the television age, the more our experience of history-in-the-making is derived from what we see on the screen. Who's to say, then, that my review of Harold Wilson's life is any less valid than the one offered by diligent biographers such as Ben Pimlott? It matters little whether the object of our observation is living or dead: if all we know of him is in the form of television footage, then we can keep him alive forever in moments of re-potted coverage. I've never met Palmerston or Jack Benny, but the former seems less alive to me because he never appeared in front of the cameras, let alone record a weekly comedy show.

So, do you remember where you were when you heard that President Kennedy had been shot? A tactless journalist once asked Jackie Kennedy that question but her reply was never recorded. Now, November

22nd 1963 and other recent pasts are currently available at all good video shops, and most of the modern age comes in a boxed set. Calling it the Modern Age suggests that no further progress is to be made after the present era, and that we've reached a sort of bus terminus in the development of history. Everything after today is a flattening off of time, which can now be divided into two distinct phases: History (which happened up until about 1930 and which is mostly linear) and Archive Footage (everything after that, and which is a gigantic mess).

The big mess of pasts that we call modern times is one we can dip into randomly. Trends in fashion and music borrow one moment from the Sixties and another from the early Eighties. Each period from the last forty years has undergone a revival at least once, to the extent that 1998 is due to be the first year to be revived six months before it's actually occurred. We've entered an over-documented time loop, which can be stretched but never cut open.

Moreover, just as scholars constructed an account of ordinary life and called it Social History, so too in the Archival Era is it possible to construct a social document from the increased amount of ordinary things people now commit to camcorder. If we can say that in the past, housing conditions were bad and rickets prevalent among the working classes of Northumbria, so will future historians say of us we danced badly at wedding receptions and liked squirting water from hoses into our niece's face.

The consequence of all this is that it's easy to forget we all fade away into small, insignificant and annoyingly unphotogenic particles of dust. Freddy Mercury is as dead as Moll Flanders or the population of Colchester from a hundred and twenty years ago, despite having a new album out. If the population of Colchester from 1877 ever left enough unmixed studio tracks to justify bringing out a posthumous album, then it would justifiably stir up more than the usual scholarly interest. But it wouldn't bring them back to life.

That's why, reflecting on the transformation of an old man like

Harold Wilson into a complex package of historical analyses, I wonder if I perhaps have the more honest memory of him, addressing some embarrassed students and being so clearly and demonstrably just an old man.

GIVING GOOD HEAD-TO-HEAD

Many people have often asked me, as one of our greatest and oldest living broadcasters, why the televised political interview has fallen into the state of shocking carnage which regularly soaks our eyes today. Where is the politeness and gentlemanly exchange which used to characterize broadcasts in the past, when the likes of Sir Alec Douglas Hume and Richard Dimbleby would sit down in front of the cameras to an exquisite four-course dinner with napkins, over which they'd discuss anything which took their fancy, from the French countryside to Rita Hayworth? On those occasions, it was Dimbleby's job to gently steer Sir Alec and any of his companions away from intense chat about Derby County's seasonal form and drop into the conversation some tentative questions about the run on the Pound. If anyone felt like answering, they would, but more often than not they'd turn and look at Dimbleby as if he was an unreliable kitchenmaid who'd just burped in some cream.

Perseverance could sometimes pay off, though, and slithers of revealing information would be prized from ministers late on in the evening, once the meal was over and the floor dancing had commenced. Anthony Eden once outlined his response to Nasser's incursions in Suez to a young Charles Wheeler in the middle of a particularly boisterous bolero. The step-patterns for most of Eden's dances have only just been published, under the Cabinet's Forty Years Secrecy Rule. They reveal a man easily outpaced by a much more nimble Wheeler, whose command of Latin American dance techniques suggested a keener grasp of foreign affairs. (It was Wheeler, you'll remember, who had been the first British reporter to goose-step with Hitler.) Many political commentators keenly await the publication of the next batch of dance-steps, to see how Harold Macmillan mastered the shag.

All this, though, is a far cry from the total interrogative power wielded by today's top interviewers, some of whom are permitted the use of a sabre. The political interview today has become the source of inevitable confrontation, and MPs spend much time in advance preparing for the ordeal. When he or she arrives at Westminster, each new member is presented with an office, in the corner of which is their own three-quarter-size plastic television studio mock-up. It's in there they practise defending housing policy to dummies of Francine Stock made out of bones and carpet. In the Commons basement, there's also an interview gymnasium, which members can use to deny allegations to a team of old presenters who make themselves available round the clock in tracksuits and Martin Bell face-masks.

Nowadays though, politicians are crawling back by seeking to control the interview agenda itself. Some senior ministers now refuse to take part in any debate unless they can be guaranteed a final right of reply. Indeed, in the case of one particularly obstinate Home Secretary who demanded the right of reply to his own assassination, his remnants had to be scooped up and deposited on Peter Snow's desk in time for a final comment before the break.

This sort of horse-trading between politicians and the media has become commonly ugly, with a lot of wheeling and dealing and threats involving producers' sisters taking place many days before the actual broadcast. Insults and bitter arguments still occur on air, but a lot of them have to be agreed in advance by political press-officers. Take last month, for example; in a Newsnight Special on glass, I was lucky to get senior spokesmen from all three of the main parties on to the programme for a live discussion about the issues. The Conservative figure was Tory Party Chairman Dr Brian Mawhinney, and his Press Secretary rang me to find out how I would be insulting him. I told him that I intended to shout 'stumpy, fat cock' at him two-thirds of the way into the interview.

Normally, this sort of thing would have been waved through unquestioned, with perhaps a courtesy call to Dr Mawhinney's wife on the day just to let her know when it was happening and to ask if she wanted to come and collect him afterwards. However, this time things were different. When I rang the insult through to Dr Mawhinney's office, I was surprised to find all sorts of conditions being laid down before it would be passed by his spin-doctor (an unusually aggressive individual who once sold swear words to the Dalai Lama). First, he demanded that exactly the same insult be levelled against Labour's spokesman John Prescott and Menzies Campbell, the terrible Liberal Democrat. I immediately informed him that I felt the insult was unique to Dr Mawhinney, and that if any attempt was made to duplicate it elsewhere then the Conservative Chairman was in severe danger of being made to sit on a chair-covering more pallid than those of either of his opponents. (Recent surveys show that voters are turned off by chair-pallor.)

This last threat seemed to concentrate the spin-doctor's mind a lot more, and he was willing to concede the principle of a solitary 'stumpy, fat cock' on the condition he could specify the wording of the other verbal abuses, which were 'whoreish pansy' for John Prescott and 'overboiled chicken carcass, with a face like a tumble-dried omelette' for Mr Campbell. I accepted the former, but suggested 'ox-breath' as a substitute for the latter phrase. He conceded, agreeing that anything more verbose would allow the camera to dwell too long on Menzies Campbell's hurt, and therefore potentially vote-winning, face. I ended the conversation thinking the matter had been resolved. However, some hours later I got another call, demanding some more changes. The item could not go ahead, I was told, unless I called Dr Mawhinney either a 'stubbly, fat cock' or, and this was the preferred option, a 'stumpy, fat cake'. I held my ground and in the end we compromised on what turned out to be the eventual arrangement; I could use 'stumpy, fat cock' provided Dr Mawhinney was given a minute the following week to refute the description, with photographs if need be.

This is the distressing paralysis of argument and lips to which most political interviews have frozen today. Some attempts have been made to encourage a fresh spontaneity in the proceedings (last month's live discussion between presenter John Tusa and Health Secretary Stephen Dorrell about tax levies on pharmaceuticals companies took place within a ten-foot wide hoop of fire) but points of view are still not being advanced constructively (Tusa and Dorrell had just five minutes to cover the issues, then get the hell out. However, Dorrell insisted in backing up a minor point with some statistical examples, and ended up baking his tongue).

Yet the television news interview is still mysteriously, unfathomably, bafflingly and pleasantly influential in setting the agenda. More and more individuals queue up for the experience of being interrogated on TV, so much so that the forthcoming interviews among applicants for the post of Planning Officer and Information Assistant for the York-shire and Humberside Regional Arts Board will be conducted live on Channel Four News, with Mary Dunne, the Arts Board's Head of Per-sonnel, in the hot seat firing questions at a wide-ranging panel of Final Interview candidates. Representatives from the three main political par-ties have also demanded to be included in the discussion, and it's thought that no less a figure than Michael Meacher will be the Labour Party's candidate for this prestigious Yorkshire and Humberside Arts post. To complicate matters, one of the candidates, Sarah O'Hagan, a Project Manager from Kingston, has demanded her CV be read out first.

In case you think I'm exaggerating how important television inter-views are in national debate, you only have to look at what's happening in the town of Dawson in Western Canada. There, a five-month experiment involving the introduction of TV cameras into legislative buildings has now got seriously out of control, and the entire town council and State Assembly have been abolished in favour of a studio discussion.

The discussion has been going on continuously for four years now, in Studio Three of the Dawson Broadcasting Agency buildings in a suburban industrial estate, and such is the degree of authority this pro-gramme has that a number of unwritten studio traditions have evolved concerning the conduct of debate. Interviewees must approach the desk backwards, and doff their hats whenever the presenter says the word 'consecutively'. Senior Councillors are allowed to bring live animals into the studio when answering questions on traffic law, and studio guests can interrupt only if they tenderly stroke the hand of the person they wish to shout at and for the exact duration of the shout. The end of the discussion is signalled by the barefoot interviewer spitting on the faces of those he is interviewing, even if they are known to be hydrophobic.

The televised doings in Dawson have caught the mood of a nation, and all across Northern America libraries now buy books printed in autocue, by far the most popular format for any new reading material. Broadway even has plans to mount an autocue version of *Cats*. Among children, the fastest selling comic is *Interview AD*, a graphically illus-trated adventure yarn set in a futuristic city where political commen-tators like Larry King and Gavin Esler rule with a combination of brawn and astute questioning.

So, you see, I am not exaggerating the importance of the televised interview. But the central question remains: does this form of dis-cussion actually decide anything? The matter was put to the test in this country last year when the final of Rugby Union's Pilkington Cup between London Irish and West Hartlepool was conducted in the form of a studio interview around an enormous desk. Jeremy Paxman sat in the middle, and fifteen men sat on either side of him, dressed in rugby strip but all wearing clip-on microphones. Paxman wore shorts under his suit. The transcript for that interview still exists:

Paxman: London Irish captain, G Halpin, you've got the ball. What are you going to do with it?

Halpin: Pass it to Mooney, then hopefully on to Corcoran and down the lines.

Paxman: Well, you say 'down the lines', but surely you've got Hartlepool's Parker, Cook and Beal coming at you straight away, piling on the forward pressure with more poundage and drive?

Halpin: Yes, but if we can hold our lines, then at the very least we can set up a ruck.

Paxman: Oh come on! You've got the option of either getting some momentum going with your back row, or even trying a kick to force a line-out close to Hartlepool's line, and all you go for in this situation is the chance of a ruck? It's hardly running rugby, now is it?

Halpin: You're taking my words out of context. What I said was that, of course, we would be happy to run with the ball, but . . .

Parker (Hartlepool's full-back): Can I tackle at this point, Jeremy?

Paxman: No. Williams is off-side. So that's a penalty to Irish, and, Parker for West Hartlepool, surely the odds must be stacked against you now? Corcoran's a good kicker.

Parker: Well, it depends what you mean by 'good'. I saw him fluff a number of easy shots in the Wasps game and I think really the positioning of the ball at the moment makes a successful kick seem rather ambitious.

Corcoran: I've got to come in here, Jeremy, and take issue with that Wasps remark. The mud on the field last week was abysmal, and there's no way the ball . . .

Paxman: Look, we can talk about climactic conditions on another programme. The question is, are you going to kick the ball between the posts from your current position?

Corcoran: Well, I've done two drop-goal attempts before like this and . . .

Paxman: Answer the question! Are you going to kick it through the posts? Yes or no?

Corcoran: No. I'll slew it wide.

Paxman: Right, Hartlepool, after that pathetic fluff the pressure's on you lot to take the game into the Irish half, isn't it?

Stimpson (West Hartlepool captain): Yes, and we'll bring it there by crossing them unopposed on the blind-side and kicking it forward for a line-out. Once we can . . .

Paxman: I've got to interrupt you there because I'm joined now in our Eastbourne studio by Cobbe for London Irish, who'll be taking the line-out. Cobbe, could I begin by asking you what'll happen when you throw the ball in?

O'Shea, Henderson, Flood, Bishop, Ewington, Mooney, Halpin, Dougan, Williams, Blyth, Hodder, Wood, Beal, Murphy, Westgarth and Leach: We'll all jump for it!

Leach (continuing): . . . And I'll catch it. Then I'll pass to Cook.

Corcoran: But can I . . .

Cook: I'll drive forward past Corcoran.

Mooney: Look, if I could . . .

Cook: And past Mooney, and I'll jump across the line with the ball, and score a . . .

Paxman: Gentlemen, I'm afraid there we must leave it. We're right out of time. That's all from us. Goodnight.

Despite seven other interviews, the game was never completed. The videotape also reveals that in the course of the third interview, Stimpson had to leave the desk for twenty-five minutes with a dislocated shoulder.

FROM YOUR OWN CORRESPONDENCE

Time now to take a look at some of your letters. I make every effort to read your mail, and am frequently arrested for it. But that doesn't stop me getting into your houses and having a peep at what you're writing, and among your many concerns I believe this letter from James Fullenfowler of Hartlepool pinpoints a recent development that's been the cause of so much fertile outrage:

Dear Armando,

Long have I sighed at the increasing madness we live under in today's so-called modern Europe. The epileptic mayhem of constitutional politics in Italy, the tatty map that is Yugoslavia, the belching ignorance of Brussels Commissioners, all make me fret myself. Europe's civilized, learned and breathtakingly beautiful arts and culture too, once the peacocked-pride of humanity, is reduced to bollocks. Our idea of an intellectual high these days is paying £12.50 to shoot stomach-first down a water slide in a drizzling theme-park in Datchet. We have become moronic dafties.

But I have kept silent. Until today. And the reason I've now decided to put forefinger to keyboard and conduct visitors round my considerable hillock of anger is because that one beacon of hope amid a hopeless gloom, that civilized and proper moment of rightness in our lives, namely the final half-hour of the *Today* Programme on Radio Four between 8.30 and 9 am, is under threat on the Long Wave band due to extended coverage of the Cricket World Cup.

What do the insensitive and dysfunctionally-brained loons who run the

BBC schedules think they're doing by suggesting that literally hundreds of people like my wife should go to the sheer effort of retuning our dials to FM? Do they not understand that in some parts of the country it's impossible to do such a thing because the population there is medically incapable of tolerating these uncalled-for simple and temporary changes to daily routine? These were people who refused to get out of the way of the Doodlebug and the V2 rocket. Their corpses are as sure as hell not going to respond to the entreaties of pansy BBC intellectuals and all their beguiling techno-talk about 'frequencies' and 'other wavebands being available'. BBC managers must come up with something better, or I will personally spay them.

A similar sentiment was conveyed more forcefully by another correspondent:

Dear Armando,

I have long been a keen fan of the last half-hour of the *Today* programme, so imagine how f***ing hacked I am that the crappers in their tossing suits are going to shat all over it. Who the f*** do these twatters think they are that they can just come up and cack in our face, the arsers? If I had my way, I'd twist their hairy knackers off and stuff them up their sodding ring-piece!

Yours,

Sue MacGregor,

BBC Radio, Portland Place

London, W1.

But there was also some support for the move:

Dear Armando,

Nothing – nothing I say – gives me more pleasure in this inferior life than ball-by-ball cricket commentaries. I enjoy them all the more if rain has stopped play because that way I get to hear the marvellous descriptive powers of commentators as skilled as Brian Johnston and John Arlott stretched to the full, exerting their masterful prosey grip over the weather conditions and making nought but a squalid rainstorm vivid and amazing, even though they're both dead.

People from foreign lands may not understand our love affair with the wayward game of cricket, and may miss the pleasure of five-day-long descriptions of Englishmen throwing leather balls about in a field less well than their opponents, but for thousands like myself and my housekeeper it is the sublimest thrill.

Surely it is not without the bounds of possibility that this willow-scented joy should be made available to us twenty-four hours a day, obliterating the news if necessary? I'm sure I'm not the only one who is thoroughly bored with the infantile cock-fight of daily politics and who benefits abundantly from fresh exposure to the discipline and resolve displayed by our finest cricketers losing on the field. Here, in the face of adversity, all the last resources of character are drawn upon to transform the ignominy of defeat into the sweet-smelling triumph of further net-practice. Dedication is what the game teaches us: for years now I have found it the dullest, most pointless and static activity imaginable, infected with a tedium it is impossible to describe in earth-words, but it is only through my ruthless dedication to watching the game that I have now succeeded in reaching that peculiar nether-state of near-satisfaction which is attained from tolerating and then finally overcoming the exquisite pain of daily enduring it. I believe that this sort of pleasure should be available to everyone, though not necessarily for free.

Yours sincerely,

Rupert Murdoch,

Brisbane and New York.

I put all of your comments to the BBC's Director General, John Birt, who said:

'Look who are you? Get out of my house. You've absolutely no right to be in here. This is where I stay. Get out!'

He passed me on to his deputy, who said:

'Of course the BBC is concerned that its viewers and listeners get the service they pay for, but if we had to respond to every criticism from every licence-payer, we would all be sick and shattered individuals with the mental constitution of shot puffins. "Oh, we can't get cricket." "Oooh, there's too much now." "Oooooooh, can't you bring back the old cricket, it was much nicer than the new cricket?" Why don't you all sod off and leave us alone, and nobody will get hurt.'

He then shut the door on my face, but inside I could hear him and his other BBC cronies counting money and laughing wildly.

MONSTER-EYED BUGS

If, whl you reed thiss par tof my book, you feeel a bit wooozy the chnces r u've got one o thos bugs goinn around jus noww thit makes errything seeem rither strainge. Yu cant poot yur fingre on it, its jus that evything fleels slitely oddd, an u thinkk yur abowt to boke up breakfastt on yur newsagents dog. Yu feel wurs if ewe shutt yur eyes. Thn evythin strts spininiiningg rounnd and yuor nose streems enouf mucus to fil a bus.

Spring in particular plays havoc with the inside of people's faces, which ooze and project liquids previously dormant at the back of the neck all winter. It's a time when exotic bugs and viruses capable of coaxing a yard of phlegm out of anyone's mouth go house-hunting in the sinuses, so to help you recognize these beasts of the nose, the following is a swift guide to new germs recognized by the Government's Chief Medical Officer.

1: Russian Child

A small virus from Northern Odessa, which normally sweeps across Asia but was blown backwards this year by a freak cough from an oncoming flock of migrating chaffinches. The virus now has extensive hold of Hull and parts of the Peak District. Tiny at first, the germ lodges outside the throat and then grows in size to about the shape of a small child. It exhausts the host by demanding attention throughout the night, and then insisting on sleeping on you during the day when you should be leaving for work.

Recommended cure: fast dancing.

2: Flippancy 'Flu

A curio from Brazil. A small blue germ that lives in the eyes and makes the carrier appear flippant. By sucking the juice out of nerves in the head, the virus causes involuntary twitching of the eyes upwards as if tutting or expressing unconsidered dismissal of an idea. These spasms occur most frequently at times of highest emotional tension, such as in potentially violent confrontations with an aggressor or at the reception of bad news, eg close family bereavement. At these moments, a resigned roll of the eyes can look unsympathetic and has attendant dangers. In the 1934 war between Chile and Paraguay, an entire village of subjugated Chileans was put to death for being plain rude.

Recommended cure: masks.

3: MacKenzie's Anger

A pretty 'flu bug from southern New Zealand. Symptoms are repulsive. Victim spends first five days vomiting offensive blue pus then green and yellow bile on alternate days. Every fourteenth day, the eyes stink of dog while the ears constantly eject rivulets of hard wax down the sides of the face. Phlegm and mucus gush out of the nose and mouth like honey from a torpedoed hive, while incessant sweating, flatulence and defecating turns the victim into nothing more than a stinking bag of liquefied buttocks. I cannot emphasize too much how important it is you don't catch this bug.

Recommended cure: hot lemon drink, but your chances of getting the cup to your mouth before covering it in a coughed-up mouthful of clammy lung-gag are nil. It's awful. It really is. It is actually better to die than have this virus.

4: Belter's Distress

A little understood viral infection which causes a streaming nose and sporadic weightlessness. It is thought to be carried by astronauts and their wives.

Recommended cure: heavy tissues.

5: The Wild Bug of Wycombe

A fourteen-inch long virus that roams Buckinghamshire. It escaped three years ago from an Amersham pharmaceuticals laboratory and has since fed off berries and discarded walnuts, and the occasional saucer of evaporated milk put out by kindly Buckinghamshire people. The Wild Bug of Wycombe, despite its sensationalist name, is actually quite a placid creature, keeping itself to itself, running away from cars and scooters, and living in small family burrows on the banks of the River Misbourne. It's covered in soft fur and performs gentle acrobatics in front of children. However, if you touch this bug your stomach implodes and empties its contents down the inside of your legs, so keep well away.

Recommended cure: firearms.

6: Dawson's Impostor

A bug which enters the nervous system using deception. It has fifteen silver-backed wings which act like a mirror. As the bug enters the victim's body, it uses this mirror cloaking device to scare off approaching antibodies, who rush towards it but then see what looks like thousands of organisms coming straight at them and so run away. Dawson's Impostor can also mimic the sound of a heart, acquire the smell of liver, and distract corpuscles by throwing a high-pitched whine as if coming from the other side of a blue vein, and then scampering down an open intestine when the other organisms aren't looking. It is one of the most complex single-cell life forms known to man.

Recommended cure: not required. It's actually completely harmless.

7: Münchhausen's Companion

Related to Dawson's Impostor. Münchhausen's Companion is a bogus bug. It manages to enter the body using a forged certificate and creepy legs stolen from a proper bug it coshes and throws into a laundry-cupboard. It then swans into the stomach like nobody's business and pretends to disrupt the gastric tract. It gets away with it for a few seconds (causing the victim to think he's puking) before scarpering when challenged by the body's auto-immune system, which discovers that its DNA make-up is a hoax.

Recommended cure: security cameras on all entrances.

GREETINGS ONE AND ALL

I recently had to buy a card for a friend of mine who lost his dog in a powerboating accident. I didn't think much of my chances of finding anything appropriate; perhaps, at best, a blank card with a tastefully designed portrait of a small Labrador puppy playing with an oncoming vehicle. So imagine my delight when I stumbled upon something containing the following rhyme inside:

> Life is a big bag of surprises,
> A tin of peppermints won at a carnival.
> But sometimes life can toss us a shock
> Like the death of a domestic animal.
>
> So this is to say how sorry I am
> That Eliot gave his last bow-wow
> When a sleek and mighty rivercraft
> Sliced his head in two with its prow.

Needless to say my friend was delighted to receive such spot-on sentiments about his unpleasantly divided Afghan, and touched that I had correctly remembered its name. Before posting off the card I made a note of the firm that printed it. They're called Omnicitations Greetings Services Ltd and, according to their brochure, they offer 'a comprehensive range of rhymed greetings for every occasion, whether celebratory or invidious'. Last week, I visited their small printing press in Warwick and spoke to their Marketing Director, Bob Tedertant.

Bob explained that Omnicitations works off a computer database consisting of every conceivable situation for which any member of the British adult population could ever find themselves needing a greetings card. Their marketing system is less sophisticated, though. Thousands of the above 'Sliced Dog Called Eliot' card were distributed across the country, but apparently I was the first person to buy one. Now, Bob tells me, Omnicitations are working on targeting their audience more carefully, sending small amounts of appropriate cards to the one shop where the relevant person is most likely to buy it.

But on to their database. Searching through the files, I came across a section on illness, including a number of verses devoted to coronary complaints:

> A friend is there to help you through
> Times of trial and consternation
> So this is one friend who's sorry about
> Your fifth unsuccessful bypass operation.

or cosmetic difficulties:

> Imagine a world full of smiles and laughs and grins
> Imagine its people skipping, shouting and bragging
> That's why my wife and I are both sad to imagine
> Your sixty-year-old face now it's constantly sagging.

In addition, there's fifty files on different types of toxic inhalation, including:

> When pain and illness strikes
> One prays to a favourite saint
> But you've only yourself to blame
> For accidentally drinking some paint.

or

Of all the sorrows that fall on man
None is worse than untold deaths
But worse has happened to you both
Now your son is addicted to meths.

Three-hundred and thirty-seven files deal with every aspect of marriage, including:

You are a thing of beauty and joy
Of constant care and civility
But we cannot marry unless you accept
The doctrine of Papal Infallibility.

I left this delightful shop with two more purchases. One card is for a neighbour:

A baby boy brings mountains of joy
A cry of a baby girl is a joyous song
But this card is just to let you know
You've left all your car lights on.

which I'll post off the next time the incident happens. My other card contained a message of sympathy:

In times of trial and trouble
When difficulties turn to devastation
It's surely no comfort to know
You're under arrest for molestation.

which I'll probably pop through the Chaplaincy letter box on my way home tonight.

HORS D'ŒUVRES AND HUMANITY

Parma, Italy
23rd April, 2002

My Dear Ami,

I've been here three weeks now, and still no sign of any fighting. We came across a depot of abandoned sugar bags, and some small pools of recently-moistened sherbet, but nothing to indicate our Savoury forces are in any sort of danger. We sprayed salt over the whole area and doubled the guard on the Hams. I'm convinced that this war will not escalate into the bloody culinary battle all the politicians say it will.

I received your food parcel. The Barbary duck breast was exquisite, and I was extremely grateful for the snipped chives. You'll forgive me if I handed half of them out among the men; none of us have had any since we left Bristol in December.

Parma, 29th April, 2002

Dear Ami,

At last, some action! We came across a couple of Bad-tooths making primitive apple tortes in a small clearing in the woods three kilometres from the most densely populated district of Parma. Whether they intended to lob them at the Hams or just eat them, we don't know. They're probably being interrogated just now, poor sods. I hope for their sake their stomachs can take the barrel of garlic purée we've prepared for them.

Oh, Ami, why does it have to be like this? Can't men sit down any more and eat cheese and profiteroles together? Apparently not.

Give my love to our little Louis. Every night I look at the photograph of the three of us eating Stilton, and I cry.

Parma, 30th April, 2002

Dear Ami,

Ignore my misguided compassion for the Bad-tooths! The bastards have started their sugar attack on Parma! I'm so glad you are safely at home with our precious Louis and will never have to see the terrible things I have seen in the last few days. Men with their legs covered in shattered icing, women running screaming from their houses with their hair set in flan, little children playing cooking games with uneaten sponge inches away from their mouth. But the more I see, dear Ami, the more I know we're right to fight for the Savoury cause, and that the sweet-eating Bad-tooths will be eliminated, if not by me then by our children, the first of a new, properly salinated generation.

How is dear Louis? He must be on solids by now. How has he taken to the sun-dried tomatoes? Persevere with them, and he'll soon grow to love them like little friends. Take care, Ami, and remember to store away some omelettes for the winter.

We may start moving the Hams out by nightfall.

The Road to Bologna, May 4th, 2002

Dear Ami,

The Hams came under attack from a squadron of crazed Bad-tooths firing bon-bons at us from a commandeered ice-cream van. They drew up alongside us and let rip. A couple of bon-bons hit the guy next to me in the teeth, and he had to be held down screaming while we inserted fillings. I quickly lobbed some of our rind back at the Bad-tooths and managed to shatter their windscreen. You should have seen the disappointed look on their faces as the skin-bits landed on their laps! They crashed into a tree and died instantly, the sugar-filled sons-of-bitches.

Parma has fallen! The Savoury capital of Western Europe has been over-run by the Bad-tooths, who immediately started imposing their appalling diet on the local populace. They sacked all the grocer shops and ordered the men to start building patisseries. (I will never forgive the French for what they've done, and I'm glad that Paris was annihilated in the Basmati Attack.)

The Bad-tooths have imposed a five-mile Hors d'œuvre Exclusion Zone around Parma. Any hors d'œuvres found inside the city are taken off to be caramelized. Have these people no self-control? However, my lovely, the Hams are safe. We smuggled all thirteen thousand of them out through the night, and drove them in convoy under tarpaulins through the enemy lines, pretending they were a consignment of freak apricots. We're on our way to Bologna now and will do everything to save its internationally renowned sauces.

And so this stupid, bloody argument about food rages on into its second year. It has divided towns and cities, even families. I have met husbands fond of olives and pimentoes leave behind their treacle-loving wives to join the Savoury forces. I have seen kids ejected and abandoned by their own mothers for not enjoying broccoli. And how easily these vast armies of exiled children have fallen into the hands of the Sweet-toothed Alliance. Promised unending supplies of dib-dabs, they do the dirty work of their addle-toothed masters.

Take care of Louis, my dearest. He is our hope. Let no confectionery pass his lips, and he will soon walk tall for us in the forest of oregano that will be his rightful inheritance.

Bologna, May 7th, 2002

My dearest son Louis,

I feel I must write to you to explain the course of events which have taken the world to the brink of this dietary abyss. It may be that, God forbid, you grow up in a country where lemon-cake is considered honourable and where the tender, salty delights of anchovies or capers in brine are abominized underground. If so, then no doubt the obese, pimpled Bad-tooths who now act as your masters will have supplied you with a history of this war conveniently twisted to draw a glucose-tainted picture of what actually occurred between our two peoples. Here, then, for the record, is a proper and shameful account of all our behaviour, of how you were born into a world where all political discord seemed to have been resolved once and for all and then collapsed utterly over an apparent trifle (you've no idea how much pain that word causes me).

Over a decade ago, people came to realize their diet was both foolish and unadventurous. Cream and glacé cherries were about the most exotic foodstuffs imaginable, and for a while it seemed that the only transcendent experience available at the dinner table would inevitably be in the form of a pudding. Then some interesting alternatives gradually came into being: sesame-seeded breads, ricotta and other nice cheeses, variegated jars of pesto, seafood salads crammed with octopus, pancetta and similar unsmoked beef alternatives, balsamic vinegar, borlotti beans and, bliss of blisses, five kinds of mushroom! Nobody knows where they all came from or how they got there. But, little by little, they filled more and more shelf space in our food stores and soon came to dominate our kitchen life.

Dinners in those pioneering days were daring, succulent affairs. Never extravagant, but always deliciously beckoning the palate into virginal savoury territory. Asparagus and cheese tarts, rillettes de Tours, cuttlefish in their ink, roast chicken stuffed under the skin with cheese and herbs, things to make with vine leaves, and, of course, Cevapcici (Yugoslavian kebabs)! All of these meals will be familiar to you, Louis, since they now form the foundations of your daily diet, but you must remember in those days they felt like a rude adventure!

I cannot express in words what it felt like the first time I ate Curly Endive soup. That clash of textures, as the mouth first enveloped the bitter, leafy flatness of the endive stalks and the hot, smooth slew of chicken broth, punctuated by the sodden glops of grated pecorino. My lips were tight, unyielding seals around this tasty secret. I was afraid to swallow, frightened of losing the sensation forever, but when I did gulp, oh, that juddering, hot river of memory that trickled down my throat! It was a furore of flavours that will remain with me until my dying juices dry. It was then, if I but knew it, that I surrendered my buds totally to the cause of savoury experience.

By then, indulging in over-creamed puddings had lost its attraction. Now that we'd discovered that eating could be both healthy and fun, we held sweet, fatty foods in contempt. However, enough feeble-minded individuals addicted to gateaux and other suicidal desserts still represented a strong protest movement against this revolution in our stomachs. And they annoyed us with their whining, fat laments outside supermarkets and delicatessens, campaigning for more display-space for their molasses.

Going shopping gradually became more of an ordeal, as we regularly fought our way past these cackling, acned hordes of syrup addicts outside our deliciously smelling stores, but we were determined to preserve the dominance of sensible but interesting foodstuffs within the home, and valiantly pushed ourselves past.

This was the position we were in until about four years ago. An uneasy balance of emotions resulting in a silent, but threatening stalemate in our shopping malls. Then, on November 28th 1998, the silence was broken, and fighting broke out at a dinner party in Chelsea.

The details of what happened on that eventful night remain vague, but what is known is that it all started when no dessert was served. Instead, after some baked courgette boats had gone by unquestioned, followed by an apparently uncontroversial goose with chick-peas, the host (a successful industrialist) moved straight on to cheese and biscuits. Some fruit was offered as a sop to the two known sweet-tooths present (a tax expert with offices in Nottingham, and the wife of our Ambassador to Holland). Fruit had been considered a safe bet; we Savouries are happy to serve it washed to our guests if their dietary standards don't quite match our own, and I personally have always had a healthy respect for fruit though I don't necessarily agree with it.

However, that night the Ambassador's wife finally exploded in rage at what she perceived to be a serious omission in the meal, and hurled a bowl of wet pears at the industrialist. The glass shattered and cut him, and he fell to the floor bleeding. The others round the table quickly jumped up to his defence and grappled with the lady on the table. Just then, the tax expert lunged at his neighbours, screaming for sorbet at the very least, and punched the mouth of a respected pioneer of comprehensive schooling in Britain. By then, the industrialist lay squirming in agony beneath the table, his blood covering cracked cheese by his side. Soon all the other guests, including a promising MP and a prize-winning choreographer pounced on the tax expert, and clubbed him to death with some wooden platters.

News of this bloody incident soon reached other dinner parties around the North London area, and similar fighting immediately broke out, spreading as far as Berkshire and a thatched brasserie in Hereford. Over thirty-nine people were killed in the dinner riots, including the editors of four national monthly magazines. The dinner parties raged out of control for three days.

That week, the promising MP who had been involved in the main skirmish called for a debate on the issue in the House of Commons, but fighting soon broke out on the Terrace Bar. Within the month, the dead tax expert had been hailed as a martyr by sweet-toothed groups around the world, and hand-to-hand food-fights had spilled into the canteens of the major world parliaments, including a spectacular clash at the UN Security Council's seafood bar.

Across the globe, barricades were erected, people stoked up on food supplies (your mother, I remember, managed to acquire some very nice crab) and we all held our garlic breath.

Since then, my dear Louis, the Bad-tooths have perpetrated countless acts of unpalatable cruelty on our people, including taunting our clergy with cream horns. The world cannot be considered civilized until all of them are eliminated, and that is why I dream of the day when you are old enough to join me in this great battle of the mouth.

All my love and flavours

Your tender Father.

Naples, May 15th, 2002

Sometimes, dear Ami, I pray God save us from these abominable people. The Bad-tooths have over-run all of Northern Italy now. Parmesan and other hard-fat cheeses have been wiped out entirely, and the whole area has been settled by bus-loads of cake-loving Germans. The Swiss and Belgians are carpet-bombing the Japanese with chocolate biscuits, and at the moment all the poor Japs can fight back with are scallops.

Now that Parma is laid waste, we have thrown all our efforts into defending India. If the Bad-tooths really intend to take control of world cuisine, then they must make an assault on the East sooner or later. India stands first in line for a terrible desiccation, but if we can get supplies of cayenne pepper to her quickly enough, then we may be able to spring an enormous savoury attack on the enemy as they advance.

Pray for me, my lovely. This war is nearing a horrific conclusion.

Bay of Bengal, October 29th, 2002

Dearest Ami,

The long journey to India is ended, and we are now moored off her coast with seventeen thousand tons of mustard, which we intend to lob at the enemy fleet. We suspect they'll arrive any day now. A sackful of mustard on the face can be a cruel death but there is no alternative. The sweet-toothed vermin must be eradicated. We are using English mustard rather than French, since English has a tangy richness which the French somehow misses.

Pray for me, dearest Ami, and Louis, remember that capers should be pickled in white wine vinegar, and not the malt kind you'll probably be told to use in cheap cook-books.

Bay of Bengal, November 15th, 2002

Ami,

Good news. The Diabetics have joined our side! Last night, by a single casting vote, the World Council of Diabetics voted in favour of taking up arms against sweet foodstuffs. Despite the Diabetics' often woeful tendency to acquire sudden cravings for concentrated sugar intake, in the end the case against sugar and all the treachery it's caused them proved too overwhelming. I feel the tide is turning in our favour. Victory is within our palate.

This morning, two boatloads of mustard accidentally went off, and fizzed up in the water. A pool of mayonnaise now stretches along the Indian coastline from Puri to Chattrapur, and some of the men took the opportunity to bathe in it.

Bay of Bengal, December 1st, 2002

Dear Ami,

An attack is imminent. The Bad-tooth ships are lined up on the horizon, and we can make out the shape of hundreds of pavlovas on their deck.

May God protect us from the glucal bastards!

Bay of Bengal, December 27th, 2002

Dear Ami,

The fighting raged for four days, as one hundred thousand people contaminated each other's food like animals. Then, on Christmas morning, our plates fell silent. After a while, some Bad-tooths rowed towards us with a mound of pineapple chunks. A few of our men pulled out some meat, and they all made Sweet and Sour Pork together.

It tasted terrible, though, and we resumed fighting the next day.

December 31st, 2002

The war may be over! Last night, word came through that the leaders of our opposing factions convened a dinner party at the World Bank and agreed a common menu. It was as follows:

Starters
Peppered marzipan on a bed of glacé potatoes

Main Course
Roast shin of Lamb in a red Pepsi sauce,
with diced fondant-and-olive salad.

To follow
Boiled mackerel sorbet.

Dessert
Pork meringues in a cream-and-salami millefeuille.

followed by Marmite and a selection of French fudges.

The agreed cost of the meal is to be £24.00 exclusive of service, and it is to become the standard nightly meal for every member of the human population as of midnight tonight. Our leaders are still working out the fine details of lunch, but it's clear that a breakthrough has been reached, and horrendous bloody carnage avoided.

Oh my love. I will soon be able to come home and make pies!

January 4th, 2003, Hyderabad.

Dear Ami,

The worst has befallen us. Three days into the armistice, we moved across the Indian mainland as part of a monitoring unit supervising the dismantling of enemy crumbles when we came across the Big Chocolate Fondue. We knew one existed, but we didn't know how large. It was three hundred metres in diameter, and nearly a kilometre high. The amount of Bournville and marshmallows to keep that thing going must have drained the resources of a small country. No wonder the Bad-tooths were so keen to move eastward.

But we could see that work had been going on in the Big Fondue right up until the previous night. My dear, the Bad-tooths have duped us. They sued for peace, but were secretly planning an appallingly sweet attack. No matter. We now have their construction plans, and must set to work building a Savoury Fondue with such reserves of meat and fat that no-one would dare question its correctness.

We must not flinch from necessity, and must choose only from the purest, most perfect savoury forms available. There is glory in the course they will create.

Ami, I am returning home. I will arrive in two days. By then you will do what you must. Ami, I am asking you to bake Louis. In a paprika and lemon sauce until tender. He will understand.

I'll see you soon. Have some mushroom and dill croquettes ready for me when I arrive. I feel hungry.

BRING ME THE HEAD OF
COLIN POWELL

General Colin Powell's decision not to run for the US Presidency is one of the defining existentialist moments of late twentieth century social history. Powell had in front of him the near certainty of victory, albeit tempered by the equal certainty that his time in office would be violently curtailed by a demented white trucker with a hand-gun.

That Powell didn't opt for this memorable future but preferred instead to play out his past as a thoroughly popular and well-meaning soldier partly responsible for liquidizing a lot of Iraqi conscripts, is a profound comment on society's low opinion of reality. By electing not to stand, Powell can now enjoy the real benefits of imagining how well things might have turned out if he had run for President, and without the disadvantages that actually running might have brought him (ie a shattered skull from a mad Kansan). He's chosen a SimHistory where he can control the narrative of his imaginary biography, while boosting the sales of his real one.

Think just now who's the happier of two other men, Jacques Delors and Jacques Chirac. One, Delors, can live happily at home eating lots of St Augur and watching afternoon re-runs of 'Rhoda' dubbed in French, enjoying the knowledge that he could possibly have been a better President of France than the current one. Meanwhile Chirac spends miserable mornings at the Elysée Palace slumped over morning editions telling him he's a bald ogre with the popularity of a disease.

Here at home, the same comparison applies to the weary, winded figure of an actual Prime Minister, John Major, compared to the jaunty fun had by Michael Heseltine, a virtual one. Heseltine got to play with all the toys of office – big desks, John Humphrys interviews and Remembrance Day wreaths – without getting any of the flack. Pretending to be Prime Minister rejuvenated him, and probably saved him from the coffin waiting for him the day he might actually have stepped into Number Ten.

The message from all this is clear. We may define ourselves by our actions, but we can come up with a more fun definition by our inactions. By choosing not to do something, we keep our options open on how we might ultimately be regarded, and that's probably better than being written off for what we actually choose to be, whether it be a bad Prime Minister, a bankrupt businessman, an unreliable baker or a dangerous teacher. The less we do, the more we preserve our integrity.

That's why the saints and holies of most religions tended to be those who sat around all day making a virtue of inactivity. Monks standing about in friaries contemplating mortality are, in anyone else's book, dossers. The Buddhist in deep trance is the equivalent of the bad morning riser, while the hermit who spends forty years at the top of a pillar in the desert simply has a bad attitude to work – nothing a good kicking wouldn't sort out. Most saints happily cultivated rules of life on the importance of non-aggressive behaviour principally because they didn't have any children: give a shaman a four-year-old and watch whether he moralizes on 'being good unto others' or starts clipping kids round the ear, proclaiming pieties on how once in a while doesn't do them any harm.

Maybe by doing nothing we can enter that pantheon of the beatified who attained moral greatness through shirking. One day, altars and friezes will be built depicting the gargantuan efforts of a people who decided at the last minute not to go ahead with the construction of a cathedral. Archaeologists will discover the remains of a cancelled pyramid, while the Seven Wonders of the Ancient World will be overshadowed by the glories of fifteen other Wonders that people never get around to.

Maybe somewhere there exists a Chronicle of Inactivity, a fully comprehensive account of what might have been if only certain people had chosen to go ahead with certain things. It would contain biographies of such notables as Paulo Fancetti, a Tuscan fruiterer who would have gone on to be a considerably successful fascist dictator if he hadn't decided in 1922 not to stand in local council elections but instead to concentrate on his family fruit business. It would list all the possible Secretary Generals of the United Nations, and describe the voyage round Cape Horn potential explorer Stamford Reilly would have made had he not gone into teaching.

We have only one past, but many futures. If we cock up what we've already done, then we limit what we might get on to do. However, by keeping our past down to a minimum, our future can be really packed. Those malingering monks who spend their days in contemplation are probably having a great time inside their heads being President of Universal Studios, abseiling in the Cairngorms, or fighting Lennox Lewis.

The relentless sophistication of computer graphics and virtual simulators will no doubt encourage us to depart further from the real world in favour of an imagined one. Next to the thrilling death rides and astro-storms available in theme parks, we'll be going on Finance Cresta Runs, realistic computer-generated trips hurtling us through what it will feel like if we decide to go into banking.

And once all these possible futures can be laid out before us, we need never stir from our tiny cells and busy heads again.

THE PENULTIMATE FRONTIER

I'm a big fan of outer space, and have been ever since Neil Armstrong became the first man to touch the moon with his foot. Since that day, when Armstrong jumped out of an igloo on castors and showed everyone how good Americans were at chiselling rock – it was the greatest day in the history of mankind – I've been helplessly hooked on the big place. Maybe nothing can top the trouser-bursting achievement of the 1969 moonlanding but, that aside, it's been an eventful thirty years for the void, and perhaps now seems an appropriate time to remind ourselves of the most significant advances in our conquest of space.

The second landmark date is October 4th 1970, the date of the first game of golf on the moon. When 'Buzz' Aldrin sauntered back to the Lunar Module having got round the Sea of Tranquillity in four under par the world had changed forever.

Another moon hero was 'Plup' Foreman, who in 1972 became the first man to spit on the moon. This was a dangerous thing to do at the time since he had to remove his helmet. Three other astronauts had died in previous attempts. They too shall not be forgotten.

In 1973 'Cock' Henderson and 'Nancy' McPhee took part in the first fist-fight on the moon. This broke out after Henderson 'made a remark' to McPhee about his nickname when the two were out on a rock-chiselling mission. The fight took place round the back of the Lunar Module and lasted for eight rounds, though it seemed much longer because it was carried out in slow motion. NASA researchers were pleased with the results, having gained much useful scientific information about the treatment of abrasions in space.

In the mid-Seventies advances were made in satellite technology. Voyager I blasted off in 1979 with a gift for any alien intelligence it chanced to encounter on its journey, a tape containing the single most representative sound of the human race. The sound was of a Bolivian child being shot for vagrancy. Three years later, the satellite was sent back.

The Eighties saw the heavens open up with the advent of the Space Shuttle, allowing not just highly trained astronauts but scientists, researchers, foreigners and teachers the chance to get killed. In 1985, Panamanian Shuttle member Romiro Santigo officially became the ugliest man in space (he had three lips), while ambitious space-walks and repair missions were fast becoming the norm. In 1988 fifteen crew members left the confines of the shuttle to link up and perform the first Mexican Wave in space, while a 1990 crew repaired the underside of a damaged Vauxhall Cavalier which had been sent up specifically for this mission a month before.

1994 saw the launch of the first Catholic Space Station, funded by the Vatican to carry out vital metaphysical experiments until well into the next century. Within its first year in space, it had tested the effects of weightlessness on prayer (initial data suggested it gets louder), and examined what happens to the soul not only when it leaves the body but also when it starts orbiting it. Floating priests analyzed the behaviour of mice in a moral vacuum and in an expensive act of symbolic unity in 1996, docked with a Church of England Space Shuttle.

Meanwhile, man gazed out on the heavens and pondered the riddles of the cosmos. How old is light? At what temperature does time evaporate? Does space have a smell? This last question was answered in 1993 when the Hubble Telescope turned its lenses on a cluster of black holes. A black hole is a star that has collapsed in on itself with such force that nothing can escape its gravitational pull. Stephen

Hawking had earlier demonstrated that they were black because they sucked the shadows off passing faraway objects. What the Hubble Telescope revealed, however, was that there was one property that could withstand the attractive power of a black hole, and that was smell. As an object got sucked in, it would leave its smell outside the hole. Gradually the smells would build up into a concentrated ball of stale mackerel odour, hundreds of miles wide.

Following this discovery, NASA has abandoned all further attempts at space exploration. Not because it's dangerous or expensive, but because it's potentially quite unpleasant.

IDENTITY PARADE

What is identity? This appallingly massive puzzle has to be solved pretty soon if the go-ahead is ever to be given to Identity Cards. The idea is to start issuing these cards within the next twelve months, once considerable public suspicion has been qualmed. The Government plans to do this by bringing them out as Identity Scratch Cards, which anyone can buy in the shops for a pound; all you do is scratch off the special square, and if the person on the card looks anything like you, you win some cash on the spot and up to a year's worth of free identity. On a grander scale, one card is chosen from a big revolving tumbler each week, and the owner gets to choose his or her dream identity for the rest of their life, whether it's as a Sultan of a nutmeg-rich province in Malaysia, a successful pornographer, or a major sports personality, recently retired from the circuit and opening a health insurance business in Northolt.

There's also a rogue proposal to introduce Scratch'n'Sniff Identity Cards, containing both a photo of yourself and your personal smell, but a pilot scheme recently carried out in Bicester showed this to be a non-starter when it turned out the personal smell of everyone there was of tears and semen.

So, Identity Cards of some sort are on their way, but the philosophical problem of identity has yet to be resolved. After all, what will the cards show? Already, people going through a mid-life crisis or folk in their late teens confused about their sexuality are lobbying to have a blurred photograph on their card. Others suffering from low self-esteem want their photo to be taken badly, possibly in harsh lighting. Children still developing their personality will have to have their Identity Cards updated every month, and some precautions may yet be taken to stop kids swapping old identities in playgrounds as they try to build up the best collection in the school.

Identity is such a complex, multi-pronged imponderable that there is a good case for abandoning a simple card system altogether, in favour of a more sophisticated format such as CD-ROM. This way, if you're ever arrested for football hooliganism, you can present the police with a small inter-active Identity Disc which will not only contain detailed visual representations of your physical appearance but, by clicking on a sequence of icons representing various members of your family, can lead officials through on-screen testaments from friends and relatives about your generosity, good timekeeping and sense of fun. Activate the brain icon and a psychologist from a top London hospital comes up and relates your fiery temper to a number of traumatic incidents that happened to you in a field when you were three, which can be called up if you double click on the tractor. Mitigating scenes of good character behaviour showing you entertaining at a children's party, being pleasant to a frightened nun, and carefully cleaning up around the house after being sick, can also be downloaded. The whole thing comes to £85.99, so at this stage it may not be possible for everyone to afford an identity until the price drops.

Now, torrents of suspicion about ID cards have recently been bursting out of the troubled faces of civil libertarians, who argue that having your head put on a piece of plastic is just one step away from having the rest of your body incarcerated in a salt mine for forty years. However, the collection and storage of valuable information about bits of us has been going on for some time now. Fingerprints, those once innocent laughter-lines on our thumbs' forehead, are today's deadly informers. Our blood-types can turn super-grass, DNA sings like nobody's business, while dental records are all too ready to help police with their inquiries. (Indeed, so effective are dental records in identifying the individual, that Scotland Yard has plans to store replicas of all the nation's teeth in a recently commissioned National Mouth.)

So the rozzers are on to us anyway. Most of our skin and body fluids have already been bottled, labelled and corked in the information vault so all a simple photograph will do is give the police something to laugh at when they arrest us. Add to this the promiscuous contact your name and address comes into whenever you join a book club or accept a chintz free gift offer through the post, and it's clear there's a cell door with our name on it somewhere in the prison system.

I suppose what gets us about ID cards, though, is the conclusive nature of their labelling. Our entire self, our history and our potential, frozen onto a single slip of dates and images. The thought of it. Being summed up before we've had a chance to get started. If only the damn things could be issued after we died, then that might help temper the ignominy or at least steer them towards accuracy. But short of providing explanatory footnotes and excuses with our card, that's what we'll have to endure.

The only option left will be to instill a sense of individuality and uniqueness into the way we hand them over. If stopped by an official and asked for your ID card, hand him or her a piece of hand-dyed fabric and say, 'This cloth, this warp and weave of a thousand strands, this product of the back end of ten thousand worms, says more about me and what I am as an individual, sir, with the rights and freedoms and magnificence of an individual than your contemptuous square of beggarly plastic,' and then hand over your card defaced with spit. Then watch them charge you with contempt as they look up your name and address on computer.

THE COSMIC PUNCH

Every now and then you're forced to look at the entire human race and heave a disappointed prayer: 'May God in His Heaven turn the full vigour of His mighty scowl on these idiots.' As our brains blossom with invention, and our imagination yields ever more sophisticated constructs of art and amazement, we still act like tossers. The Twentieth Century saw us eradicate smallpox, but spoil the retirement party by inventing the Bomb. It saw us join together in brother-and-sisterhood by creating the League of Nations, MTV and school language labs, and yet it still couldn't prevent us starting fights with nerve gas and inventing special camps for people who were previously our friends.

It seemed such a simple, easily comprehensible idea; don't go round hitting people because it'll only lead to trouble, with maybe half your family dying in someone else's field. Just try to enjoy each other's company because sooner or later you're all going to end up in the same mulch mixture on top of a twenty-first century farmer's potato crop.

And yet, despite the obvious, empirical evidence extracted from the finest, most elegant deductive reasoning a modern brain could extrude, that sipping tea with someone and laughing a lot is a much better option than firing bullets into each other's stomachs, we still cheerily go for the latter.

There must be a fighting gene inside each one of us, probably bigger than a kidney, and it secretes its juices almost from birth. The average school playground gives a fair indication of the innate state of humanity, being four hundred square yards in which the souls of innocence tear each other's ears off over differences of opinion about *Babylon 5*.

The natural human impulse is to make fists a part of logic. 'A' postulates Assertion One. 'B' denies Assertion One, offering Assertion Two as an alternative. 'A' proves Assertion Two false, and re-asserts One. 'B' demonstrates Two to be true by kicking 'A' in the mouth.

More practical examples of this logic are: that the behaviour of a homosexual in his bedroom can be subtly affected by having his ribs cracked open by five cheering men down an alley at eleven o'clock at night, that the darker shading of another person's skin can somehow be improved by inflicting bruises across the cheeks and back, and by arresting it, or that different approaches to theology and scriptural exegesis can be resolved by incinerating a busload of shoppers. In the mind of the assailant, fighting is a form of powerful acupuncture, a complex system of physical manoeuvres which can relieve selected conditions and ailments when applied to certain parts of the body.

There's something ridiculously special about our humanity that singles us out for possession of the urge to hit. As far as I know, no scientific investigations have shown minerals to be deliberately aggressive, or revealed electron-fights under microscopes. Clothing and buttercups don't pursue vendettas, nor does gravel or lycra launch unprovoked attacks. Animals get into barneys mainly because they're hungry, but punch for punch the species most likely to fight like an animal turns out to be the same one that runs hospitals.

And it's fun, too. Soldiery attracts recruits through the glamorous possibilities of organized brawling. People queue up to join the parade ground and battlefield excited by hardware and the chance to tear some skin. Along with nobility and patriotism, a military career sucks in a rich blend of stupidity and malice. A fine line separates heroism from foolhardiness, and campaign from atrocity. The voluntary desire to wield weapons can only encourage moments when even the most saintly of paratroopers spits savage aggro in the heat of battle.

Recent events illustrate our condition. Serbs and Croats enter desired territory, but are propelled past the boundaries of logic and sensory experience – which tells them they've achieved their goals because they're now freely standing in the land they once drooled over from a mountaintop – and adopt a virgin logic telling them they can only start devising a satisfactory legal system and civilized code of economic exchange if they rape a lot of women and bury a lot of men. Ruwandan nuns, professing a belief in the practice of neighbourly love, see no conflict between their kindly and sensible theology and hacking fatal slithers off their neighbours' chests. While, much nearer home, some of us apply a rule of law revolving exclusively around the firing of a gun into a plaintiff's knees.

One could go on forever compiling this catalogue of spleen, except I'm not sure it would get us anywhere. We're all very good at recognizing the utter arse-wrenching stupidity of our belligerent actions, and have turned commemorative silences and ceremonial 'never again's into a splendid and frequent art form. Nobody can illustrate the shock of battle better than we can, though it's worth remembering most war poets were officers and therefore drew some of their brilliant depictions of killing and arse-wrenching stupidity from personal experience.

So, I've no illusions that filling these pages with typed sighs of exasperation at our fighter instinct will do anything to stop us battering, knifing, abducting, and chopping perfect strangers as much as we already do. My only hope is that someone somewhere will agree with me a tad more than he or she would have done previously that boxing is the most imbecile, debased, and cruel of sports, that those who practise it are fools, those who manage it are worse, and those who broadcast it deserve to be put at the top of the front-line call-up list come the next land battle.

TOWARDS A UNIFIED THEORY
OF NURSERY RHYMES

Foreword by Prof K M Bomzaday, Imran Khan Professor of Applied Theory at the University of Shetland

Stefan Pazzanyami was the finest mind our country produced, even though he only emigrated here from Belarus in 1972. He was the most passionate advocate of the inviolable necessity of scientific inquiry, and produced elegant articles on why it was appropriate to pass four thousand volts through a stork to perfect more aerodynamically efficient coffee filters for a catering company. He died suddenly in September after an unfortunate mugging, leaving his last work incomplete. This was to be the invention of a device which would eliminate nonsense. He hoped to use the device to make his life a lot easier but, as I say, he got mugged and eventually died in hospital of ruptured nipples.

Though the machine was never to be made, Pazzanyami did leave behind extensive notes on his research into Nonsense Theory, as well as a definitive paper which mathematically proved nonsense could be eliminated. He was always surprised by the amount of rubbish children talked, so he based his experimental research on nursery rhymes, several hundred of which he collected and placed in jars in his laboratory in order to examine the cretinous at first hand.

The document you're about to read, *Towards a Unified Theory of Nursery Rhymes*, attempts nothing less than to isolate and measure the fundamental unit of nonsense, a feat so ambitious in its mental scope it makes visionary predecessors like Isaac Newton look like bus drivers. What you hold on your lap is nothing less than a 'Theory Of Relativity' for the Twenty-First Century, so count yourself lucky.

Shetland, October 1996

Towards a Unified Theory of Nursery Rhymes, by Dr Stefan Pazzanyami

1: The isolation of nonsense

I have always been of the opinion that the surest means of achieving proper and reliable scientific data is by the cutting up of small animals. Consequently, I have spent many laborious but fulfilling years destroying menageries in the pursuit of proper rational inquiry. My interest in Nonsense Theory first arose from the chance collocation of circumstances thrown up by one such entirely justifiable frenzy. It was a propitious incident which I now call my 'Three Blind Mice Experiment'.

I was in the process of spending a month depriving new-born mice of their eye-sight. Normally, I do this in batches of a hundred but one day, because of some sort of Marxist strike at the suppliers, only three arrived. As normal, I blinded them with a pipette of nitric acid and observed their erratic behaviour. They ran after my laboratory assistant, Mrs O'Rourke, who is married to a farmer who supplies me with lambs for my ionization experiments.

I conducted further studies on these mice by cutting off their tails with a carving knife to see if this would affect their buoyancy. I then placed them in a tank of water and observed as the liquid seeped in through the holes left in their docked backsides. The weight of water now pouring in made them sink below the surface, apart from their heads which bobbed above the water-line, spitting out four-inch high water-jets from their mouths. In effect, the mice had become living miniature fountains, and I had genetically engineered the world's first wholly mammallian garden ornaments. My lab-book entry for that day is telling, for under the category 'OBSERVATIONS' I wrote the simple sentence 'I never did see such a thing in my life.'

It was some months later, when re-examining my books to calculate an exact measurement of how useful my life had been the previous quarter, that I first noted the bizarre parallels between my Three Blind Mice Experiment and the nursery rhyme of the same name. Here at last seemed a chance entry-point to that dimension of experience I had been eagerly intending to investigate and then eliminate since I was a child: the world of Nonsense. Could it be that in the course of my legitimate animal experiments I had accidentally released a small cloud of Nonsense into the rational world and, if so, would it be possible to isolate and observe its structure before destroying it?

I set about my task with Herculean gusto.

2: Mapping nonsense

I bought the rights to every nursery rhyme I could find and then translated the rhymes into much more useful mathematical components. For example, Hickory Dickory Dock became

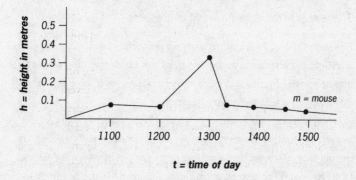

when dismembered of all non-rationality. Notice the clear similarity here with the clumsy exploits of Jack and Jill, which become appallingly obvious when rendered more clearly in graph form.

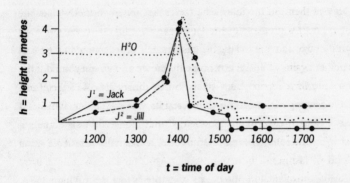

Both rhymes exhibit what I call an Upward Dip at the Crazy Mid-Point. Continuing with this method of analysis, I was able to show that all Nursery Rhymes, when smashed in the mathematical nuts, adopt a clear pattern of homogeneity. This indicated that Nonsense (N) is a constant, and I now desperately wanted to measure it.

3: Attempts to measure the height of nonsense

For this purpose, I took as my starting point the simple yet profound question: if something can be 'the height of nonsense' then what can that height be? I refused to believe there was no such value. So I then asked myself a supplementary question.

Is height a constant in nursery rhymes? Is the spider in 'Miss Muffit' as high as Humpty Dumpty prior to the commotion with the wall? Is the hill Jack fell down the same one up to the top of which the Grand Old Duke of York marched his ridiculous men? If the height (h) is constant, then all these objects will fall at the same rate, and, more likely than not, suffer the same damage and dispersal ($D<<< \ddot{\smile}$) when they hit the ground. I therefore performed another experiment.

I climbed to the top of a one-hundred-foot-high tower. I brought with me a large egg, a spider, and a small boy called Jack. I then dropped them off the top of the tower and observed them fall at the same rate. I waited an hour to let them settle at the bottom, and then went down and measured the dispersal. The egg couldn't be put together again, while the boy broke his crown and was beyond but the most primitive repair. As predicted by my theory, he died soon after.[1]

One strange exception to these results was the spider, which sat down unharmed. It therefore seemed that Nonsense was actually a variable rather than a constant, thus sending all my beautiful scientific theories crashing to the ground like a pushed pussy in a well (another experiment of mine). But then I had a brilliant flash of inspiration. What if the spider I had used in the test *was insufficiently nonsensical*? I had used a common garden spider, and perhaps the introduction here of a sensible animal had somehow disrupted the conditions of the fall.

I repeated the trial, this time with an Ipsey Wipsey Spider. It died as hideously as the egg and the boy. I had been right all along. **All nonsense has a constant height ($N=cH$).** Moreover, measuring the difference in damage done to the two spiders (one sensible and one daft) I was able to identify what I subsequently called **The Nonsense**

---

1. By the way, all you misguided champions of the nonsensical, I conducted a post-mortem on the boy to see if your beloved absurdness lives on beyond death. If Nonsense is greater than Sense, operating in all conditions separate from the carrier, then I would have expected to find the dead boy still to be made up of frogs and snails and puppy-dogs' tails. This was not the case; he was mostly bone and brains, thus proving my earlier supposition. I also tried performing a reverse experiment, stitching together bits of tadpole, leech and dog-rump to see if I could make a boy. I passed electricity through the resulting mess of bits and a mutant of sorts did stir awake for a minute or so, a hideous croaking, slithering creature that asked for an ice lolly and then dissolved into a pool of slime. I did not repeat the experiment, being mindful of the high costs of present day child-care.

Coefficient of Small Objects, (SM$_{all}$) being that value of the Objective Ridiculous within an object that makes it behave according to the rules of nonsense. The value is three millimetres, being the difference in diameter of the spattered remains of an assassinated standard spider and an Ipsey-Wipsey one. SM$_{all}$= 3⟨O⟩.

Conclusion: The height of nonsense is a constant, being as high as a hill.

4: Does the height of nonsense vary through time and space?

Consider the following perfectly good scientific logging of Ring A Ring A Roses.

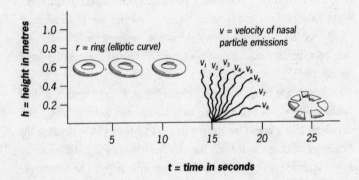

t = time in seconds

In this diagram I have for the first time been able to map through time the progress of a three-dimensional object. This is the Rose-Ring, which takes the mathematic form of an elliptic curve, obviously. Even here, there is still an identifiable pattern of descent resulting in the Rose-Ring's apocalyptic destruction at the hands of a single sneeze. (**RR+** < ≤ < ≈≈ = 🙋🙋). The graph clearly showed that in attempting to isolate Nonsense I was on the threshold of unleashing a monstrous force. However, the beauty of the mathematics involved, as well as the need to earn enough funds to pay legal fees incurred defending myself from the deceased Jack's family, propelled me to pursue my studies to the end.

In determining the height of Nonsense, I had so far considered just one plane, the vertical, and had made a very good job of it. It was now time to take on other planes and make them my puppies too. I considered time and space, and began to read nursery rhymes on a train travelling at a hundred miles an hour. Would they appear less or more stupid than if I had been reading them standing still?

My measurements indicated they felt slightly more stupid. Clearly, then, Nonsense acquires mass when travelling at speed ($N + v = N$). I therefore postulated a Fundamental Unit of Nonsense, which I called the Diddle.(♂) When approaching the speed of light, I postulated from my observations that the Diddle increases mass by 100%, (ie, each Rhyme becomes twice as stupid) thus doubling to become a Diddle-Diddle. (φ) Going beyond the speed of light, the process expands exponentially to generate a SuperUnit of Nonsense, or Hyper-diddle-diddle (which has become shortened in time to Hey Diddle Diddle). (♨)

To test this theory, I attempted to translate into proper scientific measurability 'The Cat and The Fiddle', the nursery rhyme which most blatantly uses these fundamental Units as its imbecilic building blocks. I spent the next year working on a machine that would do this for me. The resulting mechanism was a technical marvel for which I am happy to take entire credit, and involved the most daring animal experiment ever dreamt in the name of scientific inquiry: for I had determined to shoot a cow at the moon.

The reasoning was simple. If a cow could be launched directly towards the moon and propelled there at the speed of light, then the Hyper Diddle-Diddle Unit of nonsense would become operable, the cow's mass would increase exponentially and generate a stupendous gravitational tug on its udder, causing its flight-path to bend. In other words, the cow would appear to by-pass the moon on its approach and, when viewed from earth, seem to be jumping over it!

I was excited by the prospect. I was also appalled by investigations running along similar lines that were currently being conducted by Stephen Hawking's nephew, who had in a recent paper outlined his theory of Black Sheep[1] and I had photographic evidence he was building an underground sheep accelerator. I therefore pursued my own studies with the utmost alacrity, and began test-firing cows in the Nevada Desert.

I had moved there in the spring of 1994 to pursue my work in secrecy and away from the extradition officials seeking my deportation to Britain to face manslaughter charges. Over the course of three months, I succeeded in firing cows up to a distance of two miles across the sky, hurling them from a scientific cannon.[2] Several cows reached speeds of up to 200 miles per hour before crashing into sand dunes but it was hard to get one to stay airborne for anything over three minutes. They are such ungainly animals at the best of times, but when shot out a thirty-foot-long tube with plastic explosives strapped to their hind legs one begins to miss the much more amenable aerodynamism of subtler animals like leverets and penguins.

I became disheartened and, worse, fearful of exposure. Word was

1. According to the young Hawking, a Black Sheep is a sheep that, through improper dietary regulation, has become super-dense and collapsed in on itself. Hawking estimated a Black Sheep could weigh up to 56 tons but be only three inches high. If a shepherd were ever to approach a Black Sheep he would immediately turn to wool, from the inside out. Hawking has no proof these sheep exist, but is said to have extracted from a Nursery Rhyme one example of a PosiLamb (the one which is attracted to Mary and follows her wherever she goes) and an AntiLamb (from the flock repelled by Little Bo Beep) and has conjectured that if the two ever came into contact with each other, they would either cancel each other out and renormalize into something perfectly sensible, or cause a thermonuclear explosion.

2. The animals were supplied by Mrs O'Rourke's husband, who smuggled thousands of them through American customs using ambiguously lit passport photos.

beginning to seep out of my powerful rocket-cow experiments, and a local television channel had reported rumours of a cow which had come down somewhere over Los Angeles. The whole of the uptown area was strewn with mysteriously smouldering topside. Flinging all my last resources into one final launch, I redesigned the firing mechanism and came up with a space-suit for the cow which would keep its ears down, stop its terribly long neck snapping backwards with the on-rush of g-force, hitch its legs up to its underbelly, but still keep the udders exposed.[1] Wire netting towards the rear also restricted floating pats.

On a cold February night in 1995 I succeeded in launching the first cow into space. My new launcher, a catapult of elastic one mile across, was successful and the animal, Pippin, soared up into the sky and through the clouds at several thousands of miles an hour. The bovine bitch constantly accelerated at the rate I had taught her, thus reaching the speed of light as it approached the moon. If my theory was correct, Pippin would be deflected over the moon by the operation of Nonsense; if wrong, then the cow would hurtle into the rock at a speed of one hundred and eighty-six thousand miles per second, scattering infinitesimally ruptured shards of flank and gristle across the universe at horrendous speeds and maybe placing our planet under threat of a massive and destructive collision with a shower of hyperactive beef.

Of course, my Nonsense Theory was proved correct. The cow's flight-path bent slightly at an angle of 0.1 degrees and the animal passed round the dark side of the moon to re-emerge intact two minutes later. I had introduced the first controlled piece of measurable Nonsense into the sensible universe and, in confirmation of my theory, two hundred dogs which I had kept starved in a row of desert kennels for two weeks, all started to laugh to see such fun. I later heard reports

1. In space, the udder tends to float independently of the rest of the cow and is therefore a useful course corrector. Tiny rockets on the teats help to nudge the heaving animal gently back on course.

of a massive explosion in a nearby kitchen showroom, with the loss of a plate and an item of cutlery.

5: Conclusion: Developing the mathematical symbol for Nonsense

After those giddy nights in the desert, my studies reached their conclusion in the cool, disciplined confines of an underground garret in Mexico City, where I won the isolation from extraneous disturbance I required for my final mathematical calculations and freedom from the FBI. I spent six months alone with my papers labouring on the distillation of the practical observations of all my work into the most perfect and beautiful mathematical theory. I have long endeavoured throughout my life to reduce the irregular, troublesome and imperfectly patterned data of phenomenal observation and existence to the more proper and artful shape of equations. One cannot see the full beauty of this universe until one can express it mathematically in concise and elegant symbols. Equations are the most potent, the most erotic suggestors of the manifest correctness of the order that governs the universe's laws. They are for me the one, true love I can determine within. Equations are my only friends.

I was determined to uncover an equation that would explain, decode, unravel and ultimately smash the arbitrary topsy-turviness of Nonsense. And I began, as I begin all fresh scientific ventures, with an automatic query: in what way could the dissection of an animal help produce a useful result? Given that Nonsense Theory operated to one side of the normal rules of logic, it was my belief that any mathematical equation relating to Nonsense Theory must also be calculated in a peculiar way, eg through the destruction of an animal.

It was while conducting a separate experiment on some pigs in a blender for a food company interested in marketing liquid ham, that I suddenly remembered the Nursery Rhyme of the Five Pigs, about the pig that went to market, the pig that stayed at home, etc, and noted how well this piece of rubbish adopted the Principles of Parallel Universes. Could it be, I ventured, that there were not five pigs involved here, but one? One pig, but with five futures, each future affected by the initial set of physical circumstances the Pig Essence was born into at any one time. Moreover, it could be that the pig was made up not of five but of an infinite number of futures, and was therefore an embodiment of infinite potential. In other words, *is the pig a symbol of infinity?*

Turning to my mathematical labours, I then asked myself: would it be possible to take a real pig and cut it up to form a mathematical equation? If so, then the resulting mess would be the symbol for Nonsense.

I took a pig like so   =

and chopped its face up like so   = $O + o + o + O +$

The ears and eyes when re-aligned became so   = $\infty\infty + \infty +$

∞ being the symbol for infinity. Out of a pig's face I now had a Big Infinity and a Small Infinity   = $\mathbf{\infty\infty} + \infty +$

I was already on the way to a masterpiece. I then severed its snout and dissected the nostrils   = $\mathbf{\infty\infty} + \infty +$ $+ \oplus$

My equation now became   = $\mathbf{\infty\infty} + \infty +$ $\div O$

The zeros took no time at all to cancel themselves out   = $\mathbf{\infty\infty} + \infty$

Leaving me with a Big Infinity plus a
Little Infinity which is about One and A
Half Infinities =

$$1\tfrac{1}{2}\,\infty$$

So, Nonsense is what occurs when Infinity is multiplied by one and a
half and then divided by a Pig's Face

or

$$N = \frac{1.5\infty}{\text{🐷}}$$

With this calculation I am in control of the most powerful forces yet
tapped within the physical universe. Such mastery could well provide
man with a unique access to an infinitesimally ridiculous dimension,
and think of what can be achieved on earth if we can enter and
annihilate this furtive world of the silly. Here at last is a chance to exert
a neater control on our destiny, free from goblins and insufferable
pie-men. Uncertainty is no more, Mother Goose has been slaughtered,
and we will feast on her carcass. My clever work will live forever, and
will be the only stupid-less truth worth preserving. You have not heard
the last of me.[1]

1. *Editor's Note:* Shortly after completing this sentence, Stefan Pazzanyami
emerged from his garret for the first time in six months to buy a stamp and was
mugged. The stamp was to be used to deliver his paper on Nonsense Theory to
American Scientist magazine, but it was never sent. He died of blood loss from his
dugs, and the best minds have been unable to fathom his notes. The assassin was
never caught, but some lambs were spotted running off from the vicinity of the
crime, wagging their tails behind them. The President of the United States of
America has granted Pazzanyami a posthumous pardon for any wrongdoing he may
have committed while pursuing his important work, and has pledged to spend $400
billion on the quest to divide one and a half infinities by a pig's face before the end
of the century.

WRITE HIM A PUNCHLINE
HE CAN'T REFUSE

Maybe people are just a lot sadder than they ever were before, but the demand for the services of a good comedian has exactly quintupled since 1986. Not only are our Saturday nights impregnated with funny people on the telly or in unpleasant pubs, but otherwise serious outlets like news programmes, documentaries on Haiti, or newly-commissioned operas now feel incomplete without a comedian at the helm.

Only this week, Jack Dee has signed up to a three-year-commission with the Royal Scots Guards as their Regimental Comedian, while the Government has announced plans for a War Comedian to join British forces in any future overseas conflict, with the unique purpose of 'bringing back from the theatre of war ideas and observations which may contribute to a better understanding of the quirky nature of human political behaviour in specifically militaristic environments'. Both Robert Newman and Michael Bentine are said to be on the shortlist.

Comedy is now studied like a serious art-form. Charles Saatchi has bought up a number of jokes and exhibited them in his gallery. The catalogue includes Norman Vaughan's 'Mother-in-Law, with Rule of Three', expected to sell at £25,000, and an old 'Prelate and Car Mechanic Incongruity' supplied by Dave Allen. In the Modern Jokes section, look out for a beautifully structured set of 'Bee-to-Travelling Salesman Similarities' on loan from Eddie Izzard.

Comedy has convulsed into a gigantic industry sprawling across the continents. Multinationals invest millions in the research and development of new forms of humour in lands previously thought unfunny. Comedy Clubs are being set up in the Kalahari Desert and Newfoundland, while in the jungle of Sumatra a hill tribe has been discovered that may have been practising comedy undisturbed for the last three hundred years. The village is organized into a semicircular pattern of canvas huts, all directed towards a central raised bamboo platform where at sunrise and sunset the King makes humorous observations on why you no longer get those vine-leaves with the speckled stalks any more. The tribe has thirty-five different words for the concept of 'wry'.

But as the world opens its mouth to laugh, corruption comes along and sticks all ten of its dirty fingers in. It's clear now that organized crime has entered and maybe controls the comedy industry, and investigations have uncovered a complex web of connections between the Mafia and that most shady of comedic phenomena, comedy development.

Comedy development is an industry in itself. It involves millions of pounds from the BBC, ITV, Channel 4, and the Mirror Group being poured into the so-called 'development of fresh and innovative comic talent'. Youngsters of just thirteen or fourteen are pulled in off the street and shown how to satirize, programmes and pilot scripts are made in out-of-town studios and shown at night to no more than twenty-four people. Ideas circulate by word of mouth and are then never heard of again. People disappear. Thousands are employed in the business of comedy development, but none of them have at any time done anything.

The comedy development industry, it's now clear, is an enormous front, set up and run by the Mafia from a central command point in Taormina, Sicily. There, the heads of all the factions meet regularly to organize the raising of revenue through the commissioning from the British networks of pilot programmes for poor light entertainment ideas they know they'll never have to make into a series. The Borghesi family control the supply of ideas for sit-coms set in garages, police stations, supermarkets and swimming pools, while the Puttanesca Family hold the monopoly on character-based comedy, such as narratives centred on incompetent handymen, nervous air-traffic controllers or consumptive vets. The Primipordi clan specialize in gaining commissions to develop bad ideas for magic shows.

Over the years, these people have become skilled in the manipulation and control of comic conceits, so that, even though their prime aim is to secure finance for unworkable ideas, their familiarity with such a wide variety of material has led, ironically, to their acquiring the greatest expertise in structuring good comedy. If you catch him with a little too much wine in his system, Augusto Puttanesca will tell you all you need to know about character development, how the character is revealed in the situation and how therefore the situation must feel natural rather than imposed, how the subsidiary characters must play off facets of the principal character's personality which may not have been fully developed in isolation but which, when brought into contact with these subsidiary characters, can be hilariously revealed, and how the central character should have an amusing stutter. If you reveal any of this, though, he will kill you.

One such bloody episode occurred several years ago when a Casa Nostra hit man, Zezzo Marchetta, thought he'd come up with a potentially brilliant six-part series set in a bakery featuring Miles Kington and Nigel Planer as two rival van drivers competing for the same delivery contract from bakery owner Juliet Stevenson. Zezzo talked to agents and channel controllers, who all liked what they heard, and then wrote one full episode and treatments for the remaining five. Against Mafia rules, he recorded a pilot show in Teddington and won a thirteen-part series commission from Carlton Television. It was called *The Competing Vans*.

The Mafia, aware that their lucrative and carefully regulated system of deliberately unsuccessful comedy was about to be blown apart, moved swiftly. The night before the start of recording, Miles Kington and Nigel Planer were knocked down by a runaway hovercraft whose controls had been tampered with, while Juliet Stevenson returned to her flat to discover a hundred children inside daubing her walls with meat. Zezzo Machetto's throat was ripped from his body and subsequently re-inserted, though not via his mouth. As he lay dying in a pool of his own tonsils, Zezzo gurgled one last profound statement. 'There are two golden rules of comedy,' he spewed. 'Rule One is always leave your audience wanting more.' Then he died.

The Competing Vans did not get made, and to this day the Mafia exerts its bloody grip on the throat that is the klondike of British laughter.

MY FAVOURITE DICTATORS

As China's frail and gibbering supremo Deng Xiaoping hits his mid-nineties, still flapping stupidly around like a wasp in October, it's interesting to note that even now he commands utter authority in that land though he holds no official position in the Chinese Government. Despite his reported inability to speak, hear, see or think, Deng's every bodily function is granted the status of edict. The slightest dribble can lead to the construction of a fifty-billion-dollar dam, while a hundred dissidents may be shot at the merest crack of a hip.

Compare his aura of command with the one that still fails to surround Bill Clinton, a fresh-faced young man with a healthy libido and with his fingers (all of them working) on bigger buttons. Despite an American economic boom and an extended stay in office, there's still a devastating perception of indecisiveness and lack of backbone in Clinton which occasionally leads to his Administration's authority collapsing faster than Felicity Kendal's face.

So how exactly does one acquire authority? My old Latin teacher Mr Franken had it while my Maths teacher Mr Henderson hadn't. Mr Franken would simply stare a rampaging pupil into submission with a casual look while Mr Henderson could administer physical punishments until the collapse of the core curriculum and still get pelted with pre-pubescent phlegm. It seems you're either born with the word 'Authority' tattooed on your skin or you're not. Knowledge of this fact from an early stage would be a dangerous thing. It could so easily have spurred Mr Franken on to conquer half of Europe instead of just teaching us about how the Romans did.

On a more national level, John Major must surely have worked out this basic difference between himself and his predecessor. Margaret Thatcher always won our submission, though people knew at the time that what she was up to was objectively rubbish. Everyone raised their quibbles about the organized destruction of Britain's manufacturing base, the creation of an underclass big enough to fill eighteen Center Parcs, and the logical inconsistency of saying there was no such thing as society while being enormously keen to release psychopathic schizophrenics back into it.

Yet the nation still voted for her in a series of regular involuntary spasms throughout the Eighties. At the moment of voting some basic, primeval impulse took hold of Britain's brains when pencil was put to traceless slip. Even Labour MPs were known to go into polling booths on election day, believe the Tory posters about Labour's tax plans, and quietly vote themselves out of Parliament.

After Thatcher, by unanimous agreement, the Conservatives had a puddle as leader, and their supporters consequently went into hiding, like Nazis in Paraguay. Identities were disguised through plastic surgery, and the shame of past misdeeds erased. It is now easier to capture a man of the calibre of Carlos the Jackal than to get someone to admit voting Conservative in the last election. This despite an economic outlook that most experts agree smells, if not of roses, then of parsley.

People like the idea of someone who tells them what to do. We like to have decisions made for us, even if they're screamingly bad ones, since it's still a lot less bother than having to make them ourselves. Anybody who can make more decisions, faster decisions and louder decisions than anyone else gets our vote. It doesn't matter that a leader's response to the first threat of armed invasion is to order all four year olds into a line across the south coast and get them to piss a huge canal in front of the enemy, if that order is given swiftly and confidently and within seconds of the initial threat, we will all quite happily put our sons and daughters into the first train to Dover with a bag of citrus fruits.

Those who run micro and macro economies are also enormously impressed by leaders. Hence the buckets of wonga company managers are happy to pay for their employees to attend management training courses on Leadership Skills run by the likes of Will Carling or the British Swimming Squad. Will Carling is someone who's very good at organizing a group of bulky men to pass an oval bladder about a field successfully, and yet British Industry seems only too anxious to try introducing some of these skills into the boardroom. Why?

Perhaps the reason lies in our meek relationship with these authoritative people. Management pays for such excitement because otherwise what is management other than an essentially dull and uneventful set of circumstances that blights a frighteningly high number of people's lives? Management encourages most unfortunates to live a life of unattainable ambition within a make-believe hierarchy, and appeases disappointed hopes by giving out little parcels of responsibility to those who are slightly fat. Management is a permanent reminder that you are not ultimately in charge of your own destiny, that you will never run with the wind in your hair across freshly-harvested cornfields, that your hopes of maybe one day opening a restaurant or just a record shop are now charred ash, that you have no understanding of, contact with or even liking for late teens to mid-twenties culture and that your idea of having a good time is eating a Red Leicester Ploughman's with some of the boys from the squash ladder.

Managers are widespread and workaday. Leaders and heroes aren't. Which is why we're happy to let them get on with it, whether launching a nuclear assault or showing us how forming a scrum can help a board meeting come to a quick decision on marketing strategy.

Meanwhile, in a small hidden city kept private for his own use, dictators like Deng sit ordering billions of people about ultimately because he knows we can't be fagged clearing our mess up ourselves. Leaders who try winning votes by promising to 'consult' with the people before reaching any momentous decisions have only themselves to blame when the words 'You tell us, mate' come back to their In Tray. As Conservative and Labour leaders jettison policy in favour of in-depth surveys into what the people want, they may like to pause to consider that what the people really want is for them to behave a bit more like a ninety-four-year-old Chinaman with bowel trouble, for that, ultimately, is who we want from our democracy. And if he's played at Wembley then even better.

RECOMMENDATIONS ON
THE NON-CONTACT TACKLING
OF VIOLENCE IN SPORT

I've been asked by Parliament to conduct a full public inquiry into the spread of violence in sport and these are my committee's preliminary findings.

1: Perimeter fencing

There needs to be a lot more of it. Last month's scenes at the World Snooker championships in Sheffield would not have happened had sufficiently strong barriers been constructed around the playing area. Over fourteen people managed to invade the table, and could only be dispersed through the use of a mounted policeman. There was one fatality, and an injured horse.

2: Violence by players

This too is on the increase. It is not uncommon now for football players to leave the field mid-game and organize the contract killing of a spectator through the use of a hired marksman and false number-plated getaway car hidden in the stand, while laundering payment money through a number of off-shore deposit and investment funds during the half-time interval. Players known to be involved in such activity should face a mandatory suspension of six months, this sentence to be suspended for six months. Players guilty of lesser infringements on the pitch – punching, biting, puking, tugging, phlegming, licking or roaring – should be fined heavily and have perimeter fencing placed around them for the rest of the game.

3: Dangerous sports

The committee accepts that danger is an inherent part of some sports such as motor racing or curling and that to remove the element of risk totally from these sports would be like removing all the fingers from both hands of a top veterinary surgeon and then asking him to help out in the lambing season. We certainly don't want to get into that situation if we can avoid it. However, the committee feels that steps could be made to minimize unnecessary risks. Motor racing could be just as competitive but at a slightly reduced pace if one wheel was removed from each car. Bob sleighing could occur on a gravel track, while the risk of shot-putters making a wayward throw into the spectators' area could be avoided if the put used in each throw was increased in size to about three feet in diameter. Small-bore rifles could be fitted with slower bullets.

4: Boxing

Again, the committee appreciates that some degree of violence in this sport is immensely pleasurable, and that if the practice were totally neutered, followers would channel their aggression into illegal sports such as bee fighting.

However, steps must be taken immediately to curtail the risks to the person if boxing is to continue in this country. One approach is the re-introduction of shadow boxing as a professional sport. This is no longer the seedy activity it once was, where bare-knuckle shadow boxing was common throughout Hertfordshire. Nowadays, shadow boxing has won some recognition at amateur status. Indeed, one shadow, a small, greyish one attached to a man in Leicester, has gone on to participate with some success in international bouts against several formidable fleshed opponents.

Other safety procedures for boxing may be available. For example, new technology may soon make it possible for a bout to take place in which each boxer performs his fight separately. At the toss of a coin, the boxer selected to go first will enter the ring, and perform his bout based on the fighting tactics his trainer worked out prior to the contest. A video is made of his fight and played to his opponent, who then responds to the moves with his own counter-punches. If he calculates that a certain manoeuvre on the video would have been powerful enough to have knocked him over, then he is legally obliged to lie on the floor and remain there until he thinks the effect of the punch would have worn off. The winner is the fighter who spots the least number of effective punches in his opponent's video.

Though this technology is some way off, my committee is interested in immediately implementing its principle of non-contact fighting. Taking our cue from fox-friendly fox-hunting, where a scented rag is used in place of a fox, we believe that it would be possible to have boxers fight large rags, soaked in sweat, blood, torn skin, bone fragments and urine to simulate the sensory effect of another professional boxer.

5: Blood sports

The Committee sees no reason why live animals should continue to be used in these sports. People get as much fun from clay pigeon shooting as they do from liquidating real wildlife, and so the same principle should be applied to fox-hunting. From now on, it will be legal only to hunt a clay fox. The clay fox will be given a one hundred metres head start before the hounds are released.

If this arrangement proves successful, the Committee will also seek the introduction of clay fishing by the end of the year.

SOME EVERYDAY BIZARRE PHENOMENA

For some years I've been collecting the strange testimony of those lucky enough to witness bizarre phenomena while out walking in the country. Their statements are collected for the first time here to impress you. I think they provide conclusive proof of the existence of the Strange. It may be that the world is made up not only of a plane of reality and an intersecting plane of perception but that these two planes buckle slightly at their meeting point, to form something I call The Kink of Phenomenal Mishap. Hence the title of my new book, *I Think There's a Kink of Phenomenal Mishap* (Michael Joseph, £7.99), which I ghost-wrote for Julia Carling.

The first testimony comes from Ludovik Connolly, a large jockey in the village of Edgington:

We were all out walking one night when suddenly we heard this loud gurgling sound coming from nearby taps. It was a strange, ludicrous sound, and we were frightened to the skins. I ran into the house where we'd tracked the taps down and was confronted by a mysterious bath. I knew there was something strange about this bath but I couldn't see what until I eventually unplugged it. The water spiralled downwards, but in an anticlockwise vortex! Edgington is in the northern hemisphere of this planet and always has been. Baths in the north spiral clockwisely, not anti-clockwisely. Don't you see? This bath spiralled anticlockwisely. It should have been clockwise! Do you understand what I'm saying? Clockwise! This proves there are alien creatures and that they bathe.

Mr Connolly bought the bath and moved it to Thanet, where he sunk all his money into opening a major Scare Centre based entirely around it. Unfortunately, Thanet is a soft water area and he was unable to replicate any form of successful vortex, in either direction, within the over-lathered bathwater. Consequently, he's dying penniless but his story is interesting.

My next tale of the peculiar comes from Patty Helvetica, who lives in Calne. On her seemingly dull ox-scented writing paper, she says that she has evidence her home is haunted by a ghost-train. Photographs taken with a special high-density electron-filtered camera show what clearly looks like a set of clumsy metal tracks laid up her stairs and across her bedroom. And low-frequency microphones pick up the sound of puffing. There even appears to be the remains of a small siding behind what is now her airing cupboard and Mary has caught on her Camcorder the vague, shadowy movements of a phantom steam-train scuttling behind her bed and through into the lobby.

Records from the region do show that 90 years ago a steam train was in the area, and happened to be careering out of control. On the site of the house, it seems, the train rammed through a sheep and, in the ensuing mess, burnt all its own transported mail. Could it be that some psychoseismic shift in the atmosphere has projected forward in time the locomotive's guilt at this calamity, and with such force that the train-contrition has become externalized in the form of ectoplasmic sleepers?

Perhaps. What is certain is that trains have been the source of much weird puzzlement in recent times. Many Norfolk men testify to the presence of a family of wild trains in the Swaffham Woods, made of locomotives that went missing from branch lines up to 30 years ago and which have now started breeding on peat tracks in some clearings. One man has sent me a famous photo showing the blurred outline of a carriage-cub foraging for electricity.

I could actually bore you with the number of other peculiar phenomenal mysteries I've encountered. For example, David Limoge of Memphis, Wales, was said to possess a personal aura around himself that was more than ten feet thick and meant he couldn't walk under bridges. Denise Johnson from Largs has pictures of a buzzard that can fly perpendicular to the sky. Two unconnected villagers in Derby both spontaneously deflated on June 19, 1956, barely a hundred miles away from a mysterious new road that had been built as a direct link to Hull but which many people at the time said was a secret government-built runway for the air-cars of Moon people. All my efforts to establish the truth behind this has merely led to suspicious laughter from a man from NASA.

But I am determined to carry on my investigations into the bizarre and ridiculous until all my claims are endorsed by professional mathematicians. Top of my list are the unusual sightings of unidentified Venusian spacecraft which have flooded my way. Just read this: 'It was like nothing I've ever seen. A cigar-shaped glow in the sky, howling like an angry, steel caterpillar, with a plume of dense, green smoke like nobody's business.' Or this: 'We saw the Bigfoot, a large hairy biped which then turned on its side and went up in the air, a large cigar-shaped object, with metallic hair, hurtling at over a thousand miles an hour.' Or this other this: 'The monster's head emerged from Loch Ness, and then the rest of it, climbing up into the sky, a 90 foot cigar-shaped object that was all wet and metal.'

There is definitely something out there, yet whenever I take my evidence to the government they say all the places I've been to are restricted, that all the villagers I've heard testimony from are stupid restricted lunatics and that the villages themselves have just recently become secret government testing sites for new cars. And when I got home last night, I discovered that the filing cabinet with all my evidence in it has been declared a top secret headquarters for Japanese diplomats, and is therefore completely restricted.

THE PENGUIN BOOK OF FIGHTS

PREFACE TO THE SECOND EDITION

Since this anthology first came out, I've been inundated with letters from readers recounting in brave detail some of their own fights. For many, it's the first time they've ever spat up the resolve to discuss in public what can be a very private emotional experience between two or four people, and I am particularly indebted to those of them who have given me permission to reprint their encounters here. Where requested, I have changed certain names to preserve the dignity of those who are still in continued fights with their original partners but who may not want their partners to know of other brawls they have subsequently been involved in.

Partly because of this book, Britain is now much more relaxed and confident about its fighting, and more willing to admit to a practice which it is my firm contention lies deeper in the gut of our family and social fabric than others had been willing to admit. Fighting permeates every aspect of our social condition, and yet we continue to hide it from the curious. Witness the sheer quantity of passages in literature which describe degenerate scraps and concussions in explicit detail but which the qualms of every generation have forced to be suppressed. I have elsewhere shown that much of TS Eliot's poetry was first written in the form of boxing commentaries (cf TS Eliot (1934): *The Four Quartets: Heavyweight Championship Edition*). But the evidence dates earlier than that. Using funds earned from the colossal sales of the first edition of this book, I have been able to purchase an 1811 manuscript of the first draft of Jane Austen's *Pride and Prejudice*. It clearly shows that bare-knuckle fist-fights were a regular entertainment among the circles of society in which Austen moved. The passage was excised from the published edition perhaps from fear of shocking the more general public unused to the frankness of the unpleasant writing. I here publish the relevant passage in full. It describes a night-time rumble on the grounds of Netherfield Park:

A large, barn-like holding towards the rear of the manor had been prepared all through the day for that night's physical disgrace, and a circle of straw had been laid down, of proper dimensions and affecting sufficient absorption of any inevitable bloodiness which the evening's battery might conjure.

By the ninth hour, seven grapples were already underway, with much hurt already being effected on the faces and giblets of the Longbourn and Bennet parties, both of whom were now being disassembled on the floor. Amidst the aggression moved Elizabeth Bennet, not a little sore from a parley with a young gentleman delinquent from Worcester, whom she had efficiently taken out with a hideous kick to his femur. But it was the shape of Mr Darcy she was most keen to single out for particular drubbing, and this desired pairing was happily provided by the sudden availability of her target, who had but then fastidiously bruised an uninspiring aggressor with a sharp chair to the ear. Now freed from this paltry clash, his gaze alighted on Elizabeth, whose two bleeding eyes he had much remarked upon earlier. Mr Darcy moved swiftly across the barn and accosted his red prize:

'Miss Elizabeth, though I do not imagine you to be overly disposed towards the set of moves and holds I am endowed with, I none the less pray that you will alert yourself to the possibility of gaining much informative pain from their application and provide me with the honour of fighting with you.'

'Why Mr Darcy,' mumbled she, from lips enlarged with disagreeable contusions, 'I am all frenzy. You grant me the privilege of sparring with one who has felled ten men at St James's, and yet it would be a felicity beyond reckoning to be permitted to pulverize your vexing countenance beyond straight recognition.'

And with that, Elizabeth Bennet engaged five of her coarse knuckles with Mr Darcy's lower jaw, and succeeded in extracting from its owner both an exclamation of vulgar agony and a pleasing mound of gum and denture. He, in turn, seemed inspired by the hurt, and returned the blow upon her nose, which, perhaps wishing to paint in sound some description regarding the vicious force of the administration, cracked loudly in two.

Elizabeth, though now unhandsomely disfigured, felt then her skin met with a fist of such sweet ruggedness, a blow of such happy damage, as sufficiently marked how well she was satisfied with the thorough seeing to that was her evening's fortune.

'I am not disappointed in your brutality, Mr Darcy,' she puked with difficulty, 'for I have heard much spoken in advance by your sister of its peculiar awfulness. But what regard have you for these particular thumps of a woman?'

And with that, Elizabeth hurtled herself with full vim at her blotched protagonist and gave to his appetizing forehead a neat but momentous butt with her more practised crown. It was an elegant manoeuvre which drew the notice of the watching crowd, who well considered the sound of shattering face exquisite.

Mr Darcy gave immediate revelation to his feelings. 'Upon my word, what a cow of deepest unremitting coarseness you must be to render such crippling severity to parts of me. Would that I could be equally appalling to those parts of you that are not already flapping free, but I regret I cannot. Goodbye, Miss Elizabeth.' Whereupon he assumed the mantle of unconsciousness on the floor, and Elizabeth then freely jabbed him occasionally groinward with her ivory letter-opener, a small but valued gift of her father's, carved in the Umbrian style.

The remainder of the second edition of this anthology is taken up with further letters from members of the public detailing frankly and juicily the circumstances of their formative fights. I hope you will agree it provides a comprehensively gruesome snapshot of British culture at play, and will serve to remind us all that, no matter what our pre-conceptions may be on the subject, fighting can be fun!

THE PENGUIN BOOK OF FIGHTS

i

My first squall is one of many I received from confused young boys, whose parents have often left it to their schoolteachers to show them how to handle themselves in straight one-to-one combat.

I need to tell you about an unusual fight I had nine years ago, when I was thirteen. It took place on the Centre Court at Wimbledon, just after the Women's Final, which was won by the big girl Martina Navratilova. I was one of the ballboys, and weeks of training and celibacy had gone into my preparations for the occasion. It was the most important day of my life but little did I realize then that it would end in a ruptured mouth.

The game was exciting, and the big girl Navratilova duly won. Soon a green carpet was rolled out from the players' entrance, myself and fourteen other ball boys, girls and dogs lined up to provide a cordon for the Royal Guests, the His and Her Royal Highnesses, the Duke and Duchess of Kent. The Duke and Duchess made their way down the group, casually chatting to a selected few of us. The Duchess approached me: she was a tall, slim woman with greyish bones. She caught my eye, I smiled, and she asked me: 'Do you want a fight?'

I didn't know how to respond at first, but she helped me overcome my shyness, saying, 'Just a quick one. No grips.'

Before I knew it, the Duchess of Kent had managed to fell me by kicking the weight from under my left leg. As I collapsed, I found myself grabbing at her royal face for support. It only needed a further tug to bring her down on top of me and soon I could feel the warmth from her close breath hit my lips like heat from a recently plugged in toaster. She then hit my lips. They collapsed like marshmallow, but I soon struck back with seven blows to the stomach, seven magnificent trumpet voluntaries of pain, or so I thought.

She soaked up the blows as if they were liquidized Conference pears, and then spat them back at me. I clung on to her feet like a stupid pair of socks, but she quickly jerked one foot into my mouth and sent twelve of my teeth spattering into the good natured Bank Holiday crowd like Maundy money distributed by her big cousin. I pleaded with her to stop, but the Duchess jabbed on and on, excited by the smell.

No-one saw us fight that day, and the presentation ceremony went ahead on time. I miss the Duchess of Kent, but most of all I miss her two kicking legs.

Yours, Colin Magyar, East Kilbride.

I've had several thousand letters like Colin's, indicating that not only do up to 79% of teenage boys do battle with a woman 40 years older than themselves, but that the Duchess of Kent is an extremely dangerous and upsetting piece of Royalty. Under no circumstances should she be approached without a net.

ii

Some bleeding tussles can occur in the most degrading of circumstances, as fortunately this next letter demonstrates:

Seeing the Cheltenham Gold Cup this week brings back memories of a magnificent fight I had at that event some thirty years ago. I was a rider in the 1965 race, I had as my horse a beautiful mount called Henderson, and all of my parents had come down from Alloa to see me participate.

It was 2 pm, the race started at 2.15 and as Henderson and I made our way on to the grass, events suddenly took the unexpected and bloody turn which was to lead to me going home that day with smashed lips. For, as I drew closer to the starting post, my horse paused nervously, lifted his head and whispered 'Do you want a fight?'

Imagine my surprise when the animal then rode me away from the starting gate and led me to a small paddock obscured from the course by two large schoolchildren. In the seclusion of this private ring, Henderson dropped me on to some straw, stood on his two hind legs and unfastened his saddle. He swaggered forward and rather clumsily pelted my mouth with both hooves. Angrily I grabbed hold of one of his legs and twisted it round, pivoting the horse high into the air over my head and on to the floor behind me. I then jumped on to him, but he raised a hind leg to my groin as I landed, inflicting the sharpest pain I have ever received from an animal in twenty years of flat racing.

The grey beast clearly enjoyed my agony, and as I writhed in the sawdust I saw him start to dance very quickly in the corner, performing a clumsy jig on all fours. Carried away with his victory frolic, Henderson didn't see me approach from the side. I jumped round in front of his long head and, in petulant anger, slapped him in the face. The horse stopped dancing and immediately dropped a turd of embarrassment on to the straw. Some childish impulse made me want to carry on. I slapped him again. And again. Then a fourth slap, and a fifth. I carried on slapping the creature like some weird automaton, pausing a full five seconds between each slap. I must have slapped that horse for at least an hour and yet he remained strangely still, perhaps silenced by the shame of his unnatural attempt at a fight. Once I was satisfied with the amount of hitting I had done, I stopped and looked up into Henderson's horsey eyes. He was crying. Tears of frustration welled up all over his big hairy face and I knew I was looking at an animal that realized it clearly couldn't wrestle. Quietly, Henderson turned round and slowly walked off into Cheltenham City centre, and was never seen again.

I'll never forget that horse. But most of all, I'll never forget his crying face and four inadequate hooves.

Yours, Robert Champion, Leeds.

According to the police, illegal bare-hooved horse-fights still occur all around Richmond.

iii

My final correspondent hopefully proves that fighting is a totally extraordinary business, but painful for those who aren't built like the side of a dam.

I feel I must write to you about a fight that took place in the Surgical Unit of St Thomas' Hospital, Sheffield. My seventy-four-year-old father had been booked in to have some phlegm removed and as we entered the hospital, I was pleasantly surprised by the warmth of our reception. A young nurse stepped forward to greet my father with a kiss on the lips while another presented me with a live cockatoo. Most unusually, the chief Registrar, who is normally a deaf-mute, simply stood there, shouting 'Thank you. Thank you for coming. Thank you.'

At four o'clock that afternoon in readiness for the operation my father was taken off to be scrubbed and foiled. Two hours elapsed, as I waited patiently outside the theatre. In all that time nobody came out, but I noticed that gradually more and more people arrived and went inside. That afternoon I counted a total of eighty-nine health officials enter the theatre.

Throughout that time I could hear muffled cries and tearing of skin, and what I could only imagine was the sound of my father having his head repeatedly banged against a very hard monitor and then smashed into a tray of anaesthetics. At that point, a nurse came out with an exhausted but satisfied look on her face and, noticing my worry, came over and said, 'I have some bad news about your father. I'm afraid Dr Gillicuddy has asked him for a fight.' Immediately, I jumped up and rushed into the operating theatre, only to be confronted by the most horrible sight ever to concuss the retina of a man's eye. A pack of a hundred and twenty doctors were grouped in a circle, shouting like drunken antelopes and throwing money into a ring, while a choir of schoolchildren stood in a corner, singing songs of incitement. And there in the centre was Dr Gillicuddy wrestling on the ground with an old man.

My father was no match for Dr Gillicuddy. His crinkled body was severely hampered by seventeen large drips still connected to his mouth, but taking this into account I was still impressed by Dr Gillicuddy's technique. He grappled well, and had at his command a fine series of holds and stuns which managed to dupe his foe into making some stupid positional errors for which he was rightly punished. The elder fighter disappointed with his breathlessness, and it was a joy to watch the young pretender mop the floor up with his face. At the end of the match, as my father was dragged off looking like some ancient swab, I congratulated Dr Gillicuddy on his fine attack and collected my winnings from a small bet I had made five minutes previously.

I have not seen Dr Gillicuddy since then, but I'm writing to thank him for his efforts, for the enjoyment he provided on that day, and for his supple demonstration of the power of youth. A fact that my father, to this day, does not understand.

Yours

Audrey Simpson, Bristol

Two years later her father died in a prize operation in America. Following the death, Audrey was perhaps my most distressed correspondent, and, to calm her down, I allowed her to marry me. We now have regular bouts with two lovely children of our own, who are both on BUPA, while Audrey and I enjoy domestic violence at least every other night. She will not let me out of her sight, and this book has been written under extremely difficult conditions.

WHY THE NATIONAL LOTTERY
IS BRILLIANT

I went walking one summer through the hot, ponging air of London city, and passed the statue of Winston Churchill in Parliament Square. The stance and gaze of the dark, cast-iron Dresden-crusher were the same as they'd always been. Only one thing was different: he was wearing shorts. Enormous metal ones. I discovered from a London Masonry Officer that, because of the hot weather, all the statues in London's parks and gardens were going to be recast in moulds showing each historic figure wearing summer clothes. So, for example, rather than sitting on a stone pedestal, Queen Victoria will now be wearing a bikini, and reclining on her back in the park (possibly on a wrought-iron tartan rug). Florence Nightingale will wear marble culottes, while Field Marshal Montgomery will sport stone espadrilles and a fully unbuttoned shirt revealing both nipples, each one made from lapus lazuli. The whole project will take six months, and will cost approximately nine million pounds.

You'll be pleased to hear that this excellent scheme will not be funded directly by the taxpayer but instead will be covered by a donation from the National Lottery Heritage Fund. The Lottery has benefited British society and culture enormously in many similarly pleasurable ways throughout the last few months. No-one, for example, would begrudge the sixteen million pounds donated by the Fund towards the construction of a forty-foot-high concrete peacock fan across the Thames at Greenwich.

And efforts are already underway to use a handy fifty-nine million pound donation from the Fund to build Britain's first opera housing estate. The estate will consist of fourteen opera houses, some of them semi-detached or terraced, forming a semi-circular avenue among the other houses in Birmingham's Edgbaston district. Each house will hold up to nine thousand people, and when at capacity use, the estate will be able to put on fourteen simultaneous operas to a potential total audience of an eighth of a million. The scheme will bring enormous employment opportunities to the people of Edgbaston, many of whom will be required to sell programmes or work in crush bars.

The Lottery Charities Fund, too, has touched people's lives in astounding ways. For example, an eighty-five-year-old woman, Elaine Donnelly from Peterborough, has had her application accepted for twenty-two million pounds towards the costs of getting her about with her own, personalized national monorail system. The monorail is essentially an extension of her current chair-lift, but will continue beyond her first floor landing and out onto a connecting line linking her with major towns and cities throughout the British mainland. She is known to be very happy.

The country's obsession with the Lottery has been unfairly blamed for all manner of ills (apparently there's now firm evidence that global warming is exacerbated by the enormous amounts of frictional heat given off when using scratch cards) but why should we deny so many people such an innocent pleasure, especially one that costs them only twenty to thirty pounds a week? More should be done to encourage greater participation in this national snog with uncertainty, and I for one am glad the BBC has announced plans to supplement its Saturday evening Lottery Draw coverage with a series of many separate pro-grammes broadcasting live each scratch card as it's scratched. I'm delighted too that other organizations are planning to participate in lottery schemes, including the NHS and now the British Nuclear Fuel Industry. The latter is planning to bring out a Nuclear Scratch Card, which features a map of Britain and a big cash prize for anyone who scratches off the three areas near a processing plant with the highest freak incidence of leukaemia. The proceeds from the game will go towards building a big pipe into the sea.

The Lottery brings out the best in us. There's something charming about our commitments to charity that will make us automatically donate any of our ten pounds Instants wins on further lottery tickets. Indeed, I hear Camelot have plans to harness this generosity to the full, by bringing out a new scratch card costing £12,000,000, which any major jackpot winners may want to buy when they receive their prize money.

As is always the way with feckless mankind, there are inevitably one or two rapscallions out to spoil the fun of the great majority of the British punter-citizenship. The Lottery's perfect publicity has recently been spoiled by the case of a few individuals accused of defrauding Camelot's good offices by faking winning tickets. Because of this, new security measures have had to be enforced to prevent further cheating. From now on, as people queue up in shops and stalls, random urine samples will be taken off them by officials. To add an element of fun, though, all the urine bottles will be numbered, and all winners will have the chance to gamble their prizemoney on guessing the correct level of protein-to-oestrogen ratio in six randomly chosen test-tubes.

The National Lottery is a total and unqualified success. It has provided Britain with a much needed focus for national enthusiasm, now that the Royal Family are clearly rubbish. It has placated the restless and rioting, and has accelerated the closure of unsightly bingo halls. It's peaceful message should be spread far and wide. Once, in the muddied trenches of a stupid war, all hatred ceased for a game of Christmas football. Think now what harmony could be brought to the battlefield all year round if someone set up a Lottery stall there.

LET'S DO LAUNCH

When it came, the launch of Windows '95 blurred the already fuggy distinction between product and publicity. What made the headlines was not the merchandise itself (an £89 box of fuses that allows you to do several more dull things with your life than you were previously capable of) but the aggressive way it was christened. Billions were spent on beaming advertising onto previously inaccessible spaces such as the faces of minor members of the Royal Family or the motoring column of *Cosmopolitan*.

Another recent relaunch was mounted by the makers of Pepsi, who thought a good way to make people buy more of their product was by changing the colour of the tin (based on research showing that animals who alter the colour of their pelt in winter get eaten quicker). Consequently, millions of bucks were spent on publicizing the hue-turn in a series of innovative promo campaigns. Surgeons were paid to stitch the blue Pepsi logo onto the internal organs of patients under the knife on launch day, while for twenty-four hours, in an unprecedented example of corporate largesse, all penances given out by priests in Western European confessionals were carried out by Pepsi employees.

And now our own government looks set to take a leaf out of Pepsi's PR Contacts Book, and relaunch its troubled beef industry by bringing out blue beef in the Autumn.

Whether or not a product is any good is secondary to how loudly the manufacturer can crow about it. Products like Michael Jackson launch themselves with light-shows, helicopter-drops, and choreographed children so relentlessly that we buy their merchandise in the hope they'll just go away. Which means that ultimately, the likes of Michael Jackson and Microsoft are merely multinational equivalents of persistent gipsies knocking on your door trying to sell you a hand-towel.

The difference is, the multinationals have money. Indeed, research shows they have enough to initiate even more aggressive launch campaigns, including next year's plans by Mican Electronics to hire trained gangsters to kidnap fifty million potential customers, put them each in a darkened room and use crude brainwashing techniques and rats to persuade them to buy a new Mican Digital Personal Organizer.

Given that PR overload obviously works, it's no surprise that its application is becoming more common. Later this year, Parliament will mark the passing of a new Anti-Terrorist Act with a launch party at the Ivy restaurant in Soho, preceded by readings from the Act by Jonathan Ross and Annabel Giles. A fleet of thirty double-decker buses has been commandeered by the Home Office to drive around nine city centres and release helium balloons containing the message 'Today's the day you'll have an even more restricted choice of parole options if convicted of mainland terrorist offences'.

And, following the poor reception that greeted the publication of last year's school exam results, a PR company has now been brought in to deal with next summer's scores. The results, to be launched as 'A-Level 98', will be read out at an open-air concert in Donnington and transmitted live by closed-circuit television to similar concerts held in front of three hundred school notice boards around the country. A chart showing the percentage increase in 'A' Grades for selected subjects compared to the previous results will be formed in the sky from smoke trails made by the Red Arrows. In the evening, the Secretary of State for Education will host an all-night launch party at Twisters Nightclub, Leicester Square, sponsored by the Institute of School Inspectors, where dancing will go on to 5 am to a mixture of New York Garage and Rare Groove, and where parents can bring along their children. It's hoped that, whatever next year's results may be, they'll prove more popular than the 1996 version.

On a more domestic level, it's becoming increasingly common to use highly expensive and sophisticated advertising techniques to announce the birth of a child. On July 12th last year, one young couple in Derby booked prime-time ad slots on regional television to launch their baby Samuel, at 6lbs 12oz. A forty-foot-high statue of Samuel being born was also towed through the city centre.

Meanwhile, abroad, the birthing process has been marketed on a spectacular scale. Several world sects have organized mass births in packed sports grounds, including last week's world record delivery of sixty thousand babies induced at the stroke of midnight from sixty thousand pregnant women lying around in Seoul's Olympic Stadium.

Having a hotline to an Agency has now become a prerequisite of late Twentieth Century life. An individual with a grievance can only be heard if he pays someone to turn that grievance into a 'message'. Greenpeace, once just a boatload of grumpy fans of wind power, has now become a sleek organization skilled in manipulating public opinion through daring stunts in front of tankers. Their heightened media-awareness and ability to climb fences has enhanced their filmability, and with the resulting publicity has come power.

However, it now seems the French have learned from their sophisti-cated opponents. Wary that testing nuclear weapons on South Pacific fishing villages may rebound on them, Jacques Chirac's government has hired a PR firm to hype the bombs as a good thing. Using the latest marketing techniques, sample bombs are currently being tested on small consumer groups, who have to fill in questionnaires about how much they liked each bomb's size, noise, smell, brightness and devastation. Feeding the results of all this controlled market research into a computer, will allow the French to come up with a stylish and consumer-friendly atomic weapon by September.

A marquee has been booked for the launch.

MIND THAT MIND

I want to talk about the brain, perhaps the human body's most interesting giblet. It's an astonishing organ, about the size of a prize-winning tomato and just as fragile. It weighs only four pounds and smells like Stilton yet its neurological impulses ultimately determine our every thought, movement and choice of footwear. The merest tweek of a cortex can turn a nun into a serial killer, or a tramp into a geography teacher. The human brain is basically the world's most powerful computer, but wrapped in a face.

It's also currently the subject of the greatest legal controversy to rage around a muscle since the Bobbitt trial. The judicial fuss in question is an American court's decision to challenge the validity of the psychotherapeutic technique known as Memory Retrieval, a sort of cerebral Lost Property service carried out by helpful analysts on people who don't realize they have 'suppressed' or mislaid memories of unpleasant things that happened to them when they were children. Memory Retrieval is of course controversial. People who undergo the treatment tend to turn up to the first session wanting to cure a sneezing disorder and leave the last one carrying a gun with their father's name on it and a sheaf of harrowing memories thick enough to serialize in *Vanity Fair* (who fortunately now offer very good rates for that sort of thing).

It's a controversial treatment also because it's so unpredictable. Given the frighteningly large number of memories it's now possible to store in the brain, there's a high risk that the wrong one will be retrieved. You might go in to a therapy session hoping to 'recover' distressing memories from childhood, but you may leave remembering nothing more distressing than that the names of the two foreign judges in 'International It's a Knockout' were Guido and Gennaro, or that one day at school Lawrence Campbell came in with some camping equipment he'd stolen from a shop and everyone thought he was really hard but a week later, after thinking about it, realized he was just a fool.

There are other dangers. Under powerful analysis it may also be possible to retrieve memories not from one's own past, but from someone else's: you may go in to a session intending to talk about your dad, but leave remembering that you had to meet Pepe by the mountain before the avocados arrived.

We may soon learn how to abuse the system, by reversing the process so we can deliberately lose memories we'd rather not have. I have a particular recurring memory of stupidly attempting at the age of thirteen to improvise a 'funny' Peter O'Sullivan racing commentary at a family wedding reception in front of all my relatives only to end up running off and crying, and I'm particularly keen to get rid of it, even if I have to exchange it for a sneezing disorder. The only thing that prevents me from selling it to an analyst is my guilt at the possibility the analyst might pass it on to someone else who will go on to spend the rest of their life retching at wedding receptions.

And, of course, once memories become easily locatable privacy is soon challenged. Using the right equipment it may be possible to hack into other people's memories and alter them. I know someone who's tried this already using a laptop computer, a modem and a syringe and he's succeeded in making thirteen people think they went to school with Aretha Franklin. As you can see, these experiments are still in a very primitive stage but they may one day pose a serious threat to our national security.

The brain is a mighty tool, and its memories are its most delicate ornamentation. To grant memory the status of reality is at worst dangerous and at best unmagical. I like having memories of everything being much bigger when I was younger, of summers being longer, and of Sugar Puffs seeming like an exciting breakfast cereal. To be told exactly what was happening seems to me to undo the brain's natural desire retrospectively to make the best of some of the disappointing things the real world had to offer. I much prefer having an inaccurately remembered life, which is why I'll always fear the attention of the inquiring analyst, eager to go pot-holing around the darkest recesses of my own very unique head-sponge.

GOD: THE SEQUEL

Theology has had a troubled history. Over the millennia, men in cassocks have got into fights discussing whether sins stain the soul from the bottom up, whether angels moult in the spring, whether miracles are what happen when saints get excited, and whether birth-marks are God's barcodes. Attempts have been made by theologians to update their spiritual language and make it more relevant to contemporary life. Hence, church writers now talk of the soul as a sort of 'ethical modem' attached to the body's other spiritual software, which allows us to 'log on' to a 'net' of values greater than those stored by the body which anyway is liable to 'go down'.

What's remained constant, though, throughout this fickle theosophizing is the central supposition that God exists. It's the one grand posit behind the multifarious theological models on offer, though the Deity's precise measurements may vary from belief to belief: some postulate a cold, rational God who initiated but cannot intervene in the workings of the universe, while others believe in a sort of twenty-four hour, emergency call-out God, who can be summoned at the cost of a prayer to come out any time and repair burst circumstances. There are others still who say they believe in something, but refuse to limit or personalize their notion of otherness by calling it 'God'. Instead they use more evocative phrases such as 'Ether Duke', 'an inexplicable cough of goodness', 'plasma cavalcade', 'massive piety convulsion', 'a sort of blissful harmony of temporal energy, but a harmony that is regular, unlike jazz', 'Being-and-Nothingness Inspector', 'consciousness become cabaret', 'Eternity-Trousered Woman', and, a phrase made popular by Catholic theologian Hans Kung, 'Fat Uncle'.

Being animals cursed with the knowledge of our own inevitable demise, we mount splendid belief systems to help brighten up the dark reality of death's door. My own favourite is that of the Riddney Tribe of Southern Borneo who believe that life is exactly like a garden, and that death is a form of garden fencing used to denote ownership and keep out neighbours' dogs. When we die, they think, we're being invited to someone else's garden-party, where we shall have a good time but from which we'll probably return before it gets too cold. Illness is merely a border dispute in which the person who is ill is actually trespassing on someone else's garden without realizing it.

Whatever the terminology, these metaphors and cosmologies are being attached to a perceived reality which is felt to be greater, and a lot more interesting, than exclusively human experience. They're an admission that there's something more to life than the endless cycle of birth, marriage, hernias and death which would otherwise represent the major chapter-headings of most biographies. However, this supposition has been challenged so much of late that nowadays it's probably fairer to say we're living in a society which, if it hasn't exactly killed God off, has at least shown Him the brochures for a local hospice it's booked Him into.

The move towards a post-God society is evidenced by the dropping of Harry Secombe's *Highway* programme from peak-time Sunday scheduling, and the insertion in *Songs of Praise* of more and more 'human interest' chats with local clockmakers, at the expense of direct, honest-to-goodness badly written hymns. The latest crack in God's face occurred some time ago on Radio Four. Sunday mornings on the network used to start at 6 am with *Morning Has Broken*, a programme vigorously targeted at the 65- to 70-year-old convalescent nun and which did its job well. It was the one last place in British broadcasting where hymns such as 'God, Make Me Large In Your Eye' and 'Lordy,

Lordy, The Devil's Shouting "Bang"' could be introduced without the slightest hint of irony. But now it's been replaced by *Something Understood*, Mark Tulley's anthology of bits of classical music and interviews with sensible but meekly troubled people who have a nagging suspicion religion's just a clever wind-up. As an earthquake in the history of Britain's religious culture this scheduling change is momentous, possibly up there with Henry's dissolution of the monasteries on the ecclesiastical Richter Scale; for it is official proof that talking about God is embarrassing.

Equally embarrassing, though, are the things we've replaced him with. All alone in an arbitrary universe, with no moral certainties to guide our behaviour or at least spice it with guilt, we contrive an ad hoc spirituality out of popular CDs of monks singing on the Decca label. Twelfth-century jingles for abbesses or pre-pubescent choristers squawking the Angelus-theme from a television drama about sex in cathedrals complete today's compact liturgy. We purchase these shards of theology for the car or the home midi system because we secretly crave the atmospherics of simple and serene certainty. Convincing ourselves these certainties are no longer available, we buy the next best thing which is a record of some of them being sung by little boys in Durham Cathedral.

And as the market becomes glutted with this budget-priced polyphony, we'll no doubt start looking elsewhere for even newer and more desirable mock-ups of the spiritual. Maybe gift shops will soon do a roaring trade in alabaster altar-rail towel racks and stained-glass ashtrays, while we'll start buying wallpaper that makes our lounge look like a Dominican friary. And it's surely within the scope of current technological and marketing acumen to manufacture an entire range of fully functioning little gods, eighteen inches high, alive, furry and fully immortal (if you get the right sort of long-lasting batteries), all in the shops in time for the Millennium.

Anything, perhaps, to help us conceal our embarrassment at talking openly about something which, now we presume it to be dead, has left behind an uncomfortable silence in the gaps between what there is and what we'd like there to be.

US AND THEM

In a taxi, I heard the driver say, 'They reckon they'll put her in prison.' He was referring to a recent case in the courts, involving a young woman who had stabbed her uncle unnecessarily. Numerous mitigating circumstances had been raised by the defence team (he was just a close friend of her father and therefore not technically her uncle), and much scientific evidence was brought forward relating to her medical tendency to chop vegetables in her sleep. But still, she had been found guilty. Sentencing was due that morning. Sure enough, the taxi driver was right. Seven years in prison.

I remembered not to give the driver too much credit for the prediction. After all, he was just passing on a received opinion hammered into his absorbent taxi brain by other excitable passengers. 'They reckon they'll put her in prison' he had said. He was just reporting. That's all.

I thought nothing of it, and opened up the bookshop for the day. My car lay abandoned in a nearby kindergarten, where I'd pushed it after the fan belt snapped. I wondered how it was faring in all the recent rain. 'They reckon it's going to stay like this until Thursday,' said Richard. 'But then it should start clearing up for the weekend.'

There it was again. The casual report of someone else's prognosis. It later proved accurate, and Richard and I were able to go morris dancing on Saturday as planned.

I was beginning to be troubled. Who are the originators of all these prophecies and where do they get their information?

Saturday morning, and I'm in the changing rooms, tying on my bells. I'm having some trouble with my left straps. The buckle-thongs have frayed. Mark comes up to me and says, 'Here, use one of mine. They've brought these ones out now in a fortified leather. Look at that.' He twists his buckle-thongs violently. They spring back. 'You can hardly dent them. It's amazing what they've done.'

I thought nothing more of it, and went out and danced. But half an hour later, in the middle of a complicated eightsome, my thoughts jerked in a curious direction. Mark's new bell-strap. It certainly did the job: the bells never sounded more grouped. But what did he say again? That *they* had just brought it out. Who were 'they'? Had Mark actually actually met them?

Over the next few minutes, the puzzle in my head seemed to twist in as complicated a pattern as the jig the eight of us were describing with our feet (Patterson's Lament, done in three-four rhythm). Could it be the case that 'they' who reckoned the inclement weather would break by today and that little Stacy Mambles would go to prison, were the same 'they' who had brought out a new type of bell-harness? I lost myself in thought and, for the first time in my life, missed an alternating counter-skip.

I mulled for the rest of the weekend. In the bookshop on Monday, Richard brought me over the post. 'Just the usual bills. I don't know why they don't all get together and send us one big huge one.' He laughed. But I'm afraid I shouted back at him.

'Who, Richard? Who the fuck are "they" all of a sudden, you cocking moron? Sometimes you talk utter prick, you know?' I had never used words like that with anyone in my life, let alone with someone like Richard, whom I knew would take it personally. Richard cried that afternoon and refused to sell books.

In the evening, the rain returned. I stood in the Kindergarten waiting for the AA vehicle to come and repair my car. I gazed at the scratched insults daubed on my doors by the children and their mothers. 'Go home, car fool' said one. 'Get a life, you dancer' another. The AA man arrived, and noticed the insults. 'They ought to give these kids a good slapping,' he said. 'I'd do it.' I suppressed my rage at the mention of the now depressingly common pronoun and instead considered the significance of what he's just said. 'They', whoever they were, were obviously deeply implicated in this country's legal and penal system.

The fan-belt was then replaced. 'Ah,' said the AA man, 'you've got one of those old rubber sods. Chew up on you easily. I'll put in one of these.' He presented me with some dazzling white circular tubing. 'It's got a new type of polythene coat that strengthens the stretch mechanism. Shouldn't twang up so easily. They're just trying them out now in France, but I managed to bring a few over.'

So. 'They' design re-inforced fan-belts as well as bolstered bell-harnesses? There seemed now to be an obvious connection. Some sort of specialization in strengthening hooped apparatus. But what about this place in France 'they' had? Was that where they tested everything, including my bell-socks? And where did the legal connection come in? Did 'they' sit in judgement in France dictating which niece was to be imprisoned and which child to be slapped?

I immediately drove back to the bookshop in my beautifully purring car and spent the night there conducting research among the reference shelves which, thankfully, Richard had done much to build up over the last six months despite my many discouraging noises. I slowly searched among the plentiful arts and crafts books for references to leather and rubber manufacturers, and noted the names of the six French ones. I spent hours combing the recently enlarged law section, and wrote down on a thousand slips any unusual judicial decisions concerning the punishment of relatives. And then I suddenly remembered Richard's remarks about 'them' all getting together to post us a massive bill. I scoured our now comprehensive economic section for any information on French business practices.

By the morning, I thought I had several useful leads. An Economics

Centre in Limoges, only four kilometres away from a tyre factory. A
large law courts building in Lyon sitting right next to a cycle-repair
business. The headquarters of the Bank of Paris standing directly
opposite a shop that sold rubber swimming pools. This was the product
of just one night's research, but maybe would already lead me to my
goal. I took the rest of the week off and flew to Limoges. Richard
stayed behind in the bookshop to deal with the truck of Weldons that
comes every Thursday. From Limoges I took the train to Paris and
then on by barge to Lyon. I took photographs of everyone coming in
and out of the relevant buildings, and compiled a dossier on the most
suspicious looking French people I could find.

But I drew a massive continental blank. Everyone seemed genuinely
puzzled and even disturbed by my attempts to explain the Mambles
case or mime our morris dances. France was an unhelpful cul-de-sac
in which I was questioned six times by the police.

Dejected, and financially upset, I returned on the ferry-ride to
Felixstowe. In the bar, I sat miserably on my own, keeping company
with a large Taboo. 'What a pooh I've been,' I said out loud, voicing
one of the many shocking thought-scolds I was to torment myself with
that night. I felt I must have been mad to think They existed. How
stupid and vain of me to suppose I could make sense of the arbitrary
tossings of a taxi driver and an AA recovery vehicle operator. There
was no sense. That was the answer. Only a total idiot like me or the
Archbishop of Canterbury believed in a universal order. Everyone else
deliberately didn't get their hopes up. And now here I was, paying the
price, drowning penniless in Taboo, while Richard struggled un-
thanked back home with the bookshop, rewarded only with the grief
I gave him for trying to expand the non-fiction sections on his own
initiative, and for causing that fire two months ago.

I put my half-finished liqueur down by the other ones. I wondered
how Richard was getting on. The truck would have been and gone
now, and he would be up late sorting the Weldons into arse-shaped

piles for this month's window display. I'll ring him now, I thought.

But wait a minute. All that bickering and fighting we had about the expansion. Why had he been so adamant about seeing it through? Those law and economics books hadn't made us a cacking penny since they were bought in. And yet I had to lose a third of a historical romance section to fit them all. And suspiciously, another third got destroyed in the fire. Why? And his remarks about 'them' getting together to pay all our bills, and how 'they' reckon the weather would turn in our favour. Why did he come up with these references with such sodding fecundity? Did Richard know more than he could ever let on?

I rang him up. 'Hang on,' he said, then, after a pause, 'it's OK, they've gone now.'

'Who?' I said, surprised by such an immediate confirmation of all my darkest thoughts about the scoundrel I'd been in business with.

There was a noticeable delay of half a second before Richard summoned up a laughably inept reply. 'Oh, just some late customers. You know what it's like. You don't want to chuck people out if they look like they're going to buy something.'

'Richard, the shop should have shut three quarters of an hour ago. You can't have kept it going so long for just a couple of poofing customers, you prick!'

'Look, don't start all this prick business again,' he said, feebly. 'There's no need for profanity over the phone. Just drop the foul words or I walk from here, do you understand? Look, remember who you're talking to? It's me. Your friend, Richard Clitguard. Remember?'

I thought for a few seconds. Then I at last surrendered to the breakdown that had been knocking on my brain, begging to be let in, for the last two years. I succumbed. I gave in to the twisted sense of inadequacy that coiled around my soul like illegally erected barbed-wire. I'd finally come to realize the senselessness, the frightening arbitrariness of everything around me, and me just a tiny cretin in the middle. I felt the sheer weight of financial responsibility I had carried in the bookshop, of the inquest on the fire, and all the fretting I suffered in March when those faulty books had to be recalled.

And then I sank under a thousand disparate chimeras of fear and annoyance and confusion. Of songs in my head, of an overwhelming tightness in my shoes, of a stray thought that raspberries can often be disappointing. Whether it was the three bottles of Taboo or the quiet madness of my mental situation, I didn't care. I touched a sort of certainty. I saw images of beings in flight, of angels and archangels circling in the sky in a heavenly stacking system, all with my face on them. I knew that under the control and tight order of the day was an angel under my skin which, when torn, would set her free. Oh soar, soar upwards in madness, beautiful eagle-lady, fly away from this unreal sense, and spatter chaos from your arse! And then I wiped up my Taboo-sick.

It was a gasping, blubbing pewking wreck of a fool that made its way home on the ferry, and in the morning as we thudded once more against English side, I determined to make up for my crass imbecility and pappy autistic behaviour by going straight to the bookshop and apologizing to Richard. On the way from the port the taxi driver said, 'I got one of those ties the other day that they say you can just leave hanging round your neck for weeks and it won't look any more ragged than the day you first bought it. I don't know if that's true, but that's what they reckon anyway. French, I think it was.' I simply laughed and laughed and laughed and laughed, and stopped off to buy one for Richard.

The taxi drew up outside the bookshop. I got out, Richard opened the front door, I smiled at him and he coshed me. I fell like potatoes on to the floor. He had hit me over the head with a metal bar I normally use to chase thieving children away from the cookery section. I nearly passed out and would have if Richard hadn't then grabbed my head by its hairs as I lay floundering on the floor like a lost salmon. He dragged me across to a small exit at the back. I allowed myself to be manhandled down an interminably long and uncarpeted flight of stairs, the only sensation from that descent I can now recall being the regular clacking sound my head made as it tumbled onto each step.

Eventually, Richard, with all the fury of a demented animal (it is for this reason that I no longer allow livestock into my shop) hauled me across a concreted floor and down a small, dank corridor lit only by candles. I could not imagine or speak what unimaginable or unspeakable torture he was about to inflict on my body. I had read about people like him, in a recently organized section on true crime which I had high hopes would improve our overall yearly profits.

I braced my socks, expecting the worst. Instead, I was greeted by a polite burst of applause from a group of twelve men and women sitting round an oval and extraordinarily teak table. When the applause stopped, I looked up and saw that Richard was sitting with the clappers. Another one of them was the AA man I'd called out to the kindergarten. The others were strangers to me. In the corner was a television, with a spare portable set perched rather haphazardly on the edge of a small book-case. Two maps were on the wall, labelled 'Northern Hemisphere' and 'Southern Hemisphere'. They were imperfectly hung. Five clocks, registering twenty-five minutes past five different hours, lay on chairs around the room. A kettle, some rather old-looking cartons of milk, a saucer with a few dried-up used teabags, and a teaspoon with a moist glop of dissolved coffee granules still stuck to its scoop, sat on a tray above a small, stained fridge. The place looked like the offices of a bad taxi firm that covered an absurdly international area. On a whiteboard in the corner was written a few indecipherable remarks in blue marker pen, and the words 'Straps: New resins by Friday' and 'More roads in Austria – decide Tuesday, 3.30 pm.'

'Richard, what the tits is going on?' I enquired.

Just then an improbable phone rang in the corner. Richard picked it up and answered 'Yes?' he said and then, after a pause, called across to an enthusiastic looking middle-aged man wearing a cab licence. 'Robert, what's the likely weather situation for Canberra next month? I've got some yachting organization needing to know how much crowd covering they should be planning for.'

'Is that the Frederick's Cup lot? Tell them I reckon it should stay dry for the six days of the competition, but I'll send them a print-off from the taxi gauges next week.'

Richard relayed this precious information to Australia and put the phone down, satisfied. I collared him again. 'Richard, please tell me what you're all doing down here and why you've seen fit to scrape my head seventy-nine steps under my shop.'

'Can't you see?' he replied at last. 'We're Them.'

'Them?'

'Yes. All twelve of us. Congratulations. You've found us.'

'So, I'm not mad?' I had to enquire.

'Madness isn't something we touch,' said another, a rather smartly dressed man in his early forties who I soon recognized as a humorous columnist in a right-wing daily newspaper. 'We've no jurisdiction over opinions relating to the inner self. It's only external experiences we're in charge of. You could say that what you get is what you see.'

The others all smiled delightedly at this last remark. Another phone rang. 'Hello, Mrs Rutherford here,' said an elderly lady at the end of the table. 'How can I help?' She waited to hear the request, then suggested, 'Tell Dario and Alberto they're in no fit condition to join the squad before the start of the season. They're going to have to wait until Zurich's out of the way before a definite decision can be made by the physios, and I'll be having a word with them anyway.' She put the phone down and under her breath I could hear her whisper to herself, 'Bloody tabogganists.'

'So what do you all do?' I asked, obviously.

Richard spoke again. 'We decide what's what.'

'Is that it?'

'Isn't that enough? I mean, that's quite a wide brief when you think about it.'

'But what kind of what do you decide?' I flustered.

'All whats,' said a strange voice belonging to a young woman wearing a white lab coat. 'We hev total say in determeneen what ees to be at anyone time.'

'You,' I shouted. 'You're French!'

'Yes, Catherine is French,' said Richard. 'She's in charge of the practical development of all things.'

'Like my new fan belt?'

'Oh yes,' she helped. 'I remember your fan belt. I tested sat last month.'

'But I searched all over France for your testing site, and all I got for my trouble was a pile of loitering charges.'

'Oh, you wouldn't find it in France,' said a man in dusty overalls. 'You want to go to the South Pacific. That's where it's all happening. Huge testing site they've got there, the French. That's where Catherine does all her work. She's down there eight months a year testing everything: fan-belts, buckles, new types of cement, heat-resisteant gravel for paths up volcanos, self-plastering bricks. Anything we bring out, she tries out down there in her Pacific territories, and then she comes back and tells us what she reckons about it.'

'But what about the other things? Like the weather? Or is that you?' I said, facing the enthusiastic man with the cab licence who earlier seemed very capable helping the Australian yachting club out.

'Bang on. I've got all sorts of monitoring equipment in me taxi, temperature and humidity gauges, satellite feeds to all the major meteorological craft in orbit, and I've got a radio link-up with a network of other weather-taxis around the world so, if there's any unusual or prolonged conditions, we can all exchange information on what we should be reckoning's going to happen.'

Just then a fax machine started to spit out some paper. For the next thirty seconds some crude photocopied mug-shots of different men emerged onto the collecting tray. Richard darted over and, as the paper tumbled out, switched on a nearby dictaphone and put it to his lips. 'I reckon: Number One, obviously guilty, got that look in his eye. Six years minimum. Number Two, let off on a technicality, but the shifty bugger's still got something to do with it. Number Three: put him away for now, but he was probably nowhere near the place when it happened. Come back to him again in three years. Number Four: yes. Maximum sentence. And Number Five, give him not guilty. I reckon he's been stitched up by the others. OK, and let me know if you want all of that spread around Madrid before you pass sentence tomorrow. Cheers Miguel.'

Richard snapped the dictaphone off, and smiled at me. 'You're in charge of the world's Law, aren't you, Richard?' I said, now getting into my stride.

'That's me,' said Richard. 'I'm sorry your historical romance section got burned down but I just had to get space for more reference material in. Now I've got room to house all the legislative information from the major world parliaments, I can transmit a decision to any of my judges whenever required.'

'And when's that?'

'Whenever something has to be referred up for an opinion. Anything contentious is automatically passed on to me, and I can report back a decision within fifteen minutes.'

'So, let me get this straight before any more of my brain comes out the back of my head. You twelve people here, sitting underneath my bookshop, have total control over world events?'

'No, no, no,' said the man in overalls. 'That would be impractical. All we do is influence them to the greatest degree imaginable. We just happen to know what we're talking about, so enough people in enough important places listen to us and act on what we say.'

The phone rang again. Mrs Rutherford picked it up but quickly called to the others. 'Tom Paulin's new poetry collection. Are we saying it's a breakthrough, or is it retreading familiar thematic territory?'

There was a brief consultation at the desk. The AA man said he hadn't had a chance to read it yet, but the cab-driver seemed to speak for the others. 'If that's the *TLS*, tell her it's a breakthrough, but we'll give her the reasons later. Single out "My Family's Treason" for particular praise.'

'This is absurd,' I concluded, with more confidence than I've ever concluded anything before. 'Are you telling me that anyone who writes a critical opinion about anything is in cahoots with you lot?'

'Why ever not?' replied the newspaper columnist. 'Imagine critics were left to their own devices. There'd be judgmental anarchy. A hundred different opinions on one textile exhibition? Fourteen thousand views on a book of shocking photography? The place would come to a standstill and the public would have every right to think they could do better themselves. And if that happened the unemployment rate in central London would quadruple. No. Creativity needs firm disciplining, otherwise people literally wouldn't know what to think. So, we tell them. Anyone who takes up a post on a national journal is obliged to get in touch with me, and receives a daily up-date of our opinions on all cultural matters. I'm preparing today's list now.'

I mentioned I was by now appalled at the very notion of being told what to do by what looked like a group of moderately successful taxi-firm staff.

'Oh,' said the man in overalls. 'Pardon us for doing everyone on the planet a big favour. We're not all taxi drivers, sunshine. I happen to run my own very successful painting and decorating business actually, Mrs Rutherford over there is not just any old retired History teacher but was head of her department, Matthew writes some very astute newspaper columns with a mordant wit we're all envious of, Sarah MacGuire has a staff of seventeen at Asda . . .'

'Yes, yes! I'm sure you're all thoroughly competent,' I blurted. 'But what gives you the right to do what you're doing now? How did you get to be in charge of All Things? Is there a course you all go on, or what?'

'Don't be flippant,' snapped Mrs Rutherford. 'It's actually much more straightforward. Each of the twelve of us is descended from one of the Apostles.'

I heard everything inside me go suddenly quiet.

'Our ancestors,' continued the cab-driver, 'guarded the Grail during the subjugation of the Holy Places, and took up arms in the Crusades. Over the centuries, our twelve families built up a network of associates and power bases to protect and transfer the Holy Secrets from generation to generation, and hung out in a headquarters in Avignon. From there thousands of secret followers fanned out and ended up as advisers to all those with key posts in politics and the Church. And now, two thousand years later, we're the current wise generation; the twelve of us may live day to day in more modest circumstances than our hallowed forefathers, but we're still universally regarded as founts of confident opinion on all that matters in the world, including the law, economies and the weather. We know it all.'

'But we still work extremely hard to gain our knowledge.' This came from a rather older individual in a tightly fitting checked sports jacket. 'For example, I can now confidently claim to know more about how businesses and economies work than anyone else on our planet, but it took me thirty-two years working for Dulux Paints, twenty of them in the Small Clients Division, to get me there. In that time, I saw a lot of people come and go, and a lot of mistakes being made, I can tell you. I've seen it all. I know it all. And now I run the international markets. The world's affected by what I reckon, and governments know they'd be out on their todgers if they didn't listen to me. It might interest you to learn I'm currently working on a simpler way of sending out bills, possibly by organizing them to be massed together in a lump sum.'

'Yes,' added Mrs Rutherford, 'and I run sport. I took games a lot when I was a teacher, and I've got a pretty good eye for judging what people are like. I can just tell by the look on their faces whether they're up to the event or not, so I can reckon how well they're going to do. I'm not usually wrong. I'm in FIFA, you know.'

And so the marvellous explication went on. I was introduced to Gillian Appleby, who ran a small pharmacy in Datchet, and who it emerged was the power behind the most recent international strides in medicine. She told me that all illnesses were brought on by small changes in the climate, and could be eradicated if only people kept themselves warm enough.

Next was my AA man, Kenneth Taylor, responsible for international morality. He had a seat at the United Nations, and was currently heavily involved in the eradication of slavery in some developing economies. He also expressed opinions in sexual ethics committees.

On his right, Sarah MacGuire, a forty-three-year-old senior floor assistant for Asda supermarket, responsible for a staff of seventeen, who each could call on her at any time to supply or confirm information on the price and availability of goods within the store, and to supply change to exhausted cash-tills. A highly respected individual, with a command of figures, finance and personnel. She now controlled the international price of oil.

I was about to meet Jonathan Cooper, an extremely precocious thirteen-year-old who, that very morning, had given orders for the children that had daubed insults on my car to be slapped, when suddenly the phone went, the fax machine blurted into activity, four pagers went off, and both TV sets flickered alive. One showed pictures of a traffic jam across the Erskine Bridge in Renfrewshire, Scotland and the other seemed to be a live feed from a street carnival in Sao Paulo, Brazil. Panic broke out among the group as forty-four different requests for advice beeped upon the two maps of the hemispheres.

'What are we going to do? What are we going to do?' screamed the AA man. Mrs Rutherford and the taxi driver rushed at him quaking with rage. 'Get off your fat arse, Kenneth, and help us out here!' said Mrs Rutherford. They pulled him, still screaming, from his chair while the man in overalls ran over to Jonathan Cooper, the boy. 'What do we do, Jonathan? Please! What do we do?'

'I don't know,' he replied, visibly trembling. 'I'm only thirteen, for Christ's sake. You think of something.'

The others ran around, obviously unsure which of the many requests for information pouring into the makeshift command centre they should handle first. More buzzers, bleepers, mobile phones, terminals and fax papers registered requests for assistance. Among the mayhem, the elderly man with the tight fitting sports jacket sat with his head in his hands, mumbling, 'I don't need this. I don't need this.'

The flash-flood of calls was dealt with in ten minutes. Staccato answers – 'tomorrow', 'recommission the ballet for a different company', 'use South Africa's constitution as a model', 'a controlled explosion underwater', 'try bending the bricks to fit the corners', 'skip a generation and give it to William' – were blurted down the phone by these twelve shaking individuals, and when the episode was over they all sat down and expressed their relief in tears.

'Are you alright?' I asked Sarah MacGuire, who was gnawing the table.

'Don't worry,' she whimpered. 'We always get moments when there's too much to do at once. We call them our Squit Points. We still don't cope with them all that well.'

'How often do they happen?' I asked.

'About every twenty minutes.'

I didn't respond. The enormous awfulness of their lives shimmered before me. I wanted to leave.

'Look, I think I better set off to the hospital now and maybe get these head-wounds cauterized.'

'I'm afraid you can't leave.' The man in the overalls (a decorator called Phil who knew all about skimming, building control and how to get the best out of your cupboard space, who knew how to come up with the strongest adhesives and fastest bonding grout compound, who clearly knew better than anyone else what was what, whose command of materials and methodology, on climactic conditions, import and export trends, guttering mechanisms and the effectiveness of environment-friendly wood-finishes all pointed to a deep knowledge of how man behaved and what aspirations he had for a better life) blocked the doorway with his large frame and pushed me back into a chair. For a decorator, he looked unduly bloodcurdling.

'Now you've found out what we do, you must bless us with a reciprocal declaration of openness. We need of you a loyal act of service that will propagate the views of the group, and fertilize our next generation of members.'

'You can put a pamphlet in my bookshop if you want. I'm quite happy to have posters up, provided they don't block the revolving Weldon-arses.'

'No, your commitment must be of the most enormous physicality,' said Phil, carrying on in a strangely pompous tone which he had now adopted with some pride. 'You must cleave unto Aiden Duggelby.'

Just then a man in his early forties stepped forward. He hadn't spoken directly before, though I noticed he was one of the least capable members of the Group during the last Squit Point, crying into his trousers. He had dark, monkish hair and an unpleasant black moustache that never really went anywhere.

'Hello, I'm Aiden Duggelby. How's it going? Don't worry about the scrapes on your head. A little lemon juice dabbed on with a cotton bud is what you need. Just the ticket, actually, 'cos it's nice and clear and ointment would just mess up your hair. You'd be at it for days picking all the stuck bits out if you used ointment. Anyway, I'm really pleased that you're fairly level-headed about all this because, you see, none of us here have any children and, really, we've got to sort that potato out now if we want the group to carry on for a bit more, so we thought, well, it's about time we got out of here and settled down with some willing swans and everyone here seems to think I would be the best person to try first, so I'm leaving them all behind, and I'm looking for a wife, a really creamy one, so I can bungalow down somewhere with a family and maybe then pass on all the things I reckon through neighbours and folks in the pub and that kind of *populum*, and then, wham, you come along, and we all reckon, why not, Aidey boy, go for it, so what's going to happen is, we're going to have a ceremony now, and I'm going to marry you.'

What he had suggested was possible (I am a woman) but horrible. However, before I could even think of pinching myself out of this, the worst dream any woman ever had about the rest of her life, the group grabbed me from the chair and strapped me to a pew. They chanted incomprehensible hymns about the need to bring up children with a good sense of right and wrong, and recited prayers about tax policy. Aiden Duggelby knelt down next to me, and Mrs Rutherford processed towards him bearing aloft two papyrus scrolls.

'Behold the sacred lumps of Knowledge!' she shrieked. 'Take and scatter.'

'Bountiful will be your produce, and incisive your remarks,' said Kenneth Taylor from the AA.

'For you know, and know it all. You have the eagle's eye,' responded the group as one.

'Oh Aiden Duggelby,' said Mrs Rutherford. 'Take these your scrolls, and entrust the handy secrets contained herein to the vagaries of the numbskulled earth. Receive this thine mission.'

At this point, the scrolls were unfurled, and revealed the source of information Aiden Duggelby was clearly to be in charge of when married to me and living in my neighbourhood. It contained a series of complex charts and diagrams clearly showing that many of the songs, television programmes and films of fifteen years ago were twice as good as the ones produced today. It outlined information on hotel facilities abroad and where there could be room for improvement, which we were clearly expected to disseminate to other travellers when on holiday or on train journeys. There were comprehensive accounts of the failings of the railway system, and information on the quickest and most direct car routes for any long journey, that we were obliged to swear we would pass on at the slightest invitation. There were instructions on the limitations of the health systems of most western countries as well as a fund of suggestions on how best to keep children amused with tricks and fancy treats. Here before me, written in gold, was knowledge of how life could be lived among ordinary people in a state of happiness and confidence in the certainty of one's own opinions.

Gazing on the scrolls, I yielded, and numbly let the rest of the ceremony continue in front of me. A garland of flowers was placed on my head, and Aiden Duggelby kissed me, to a marriage pronouncement from the taxi driver enjoining me to Aiden and calling upon the powers of Mighty God to secure the line of Duggelbys (descendants of St Luke) into the next millennia. An organ played the original *Tomorrow's World* theme tune, and we were ushered out of the room and back up my stairs. Aiden and I, hand in hand and with slow, solemn tread, nervously left that sanctified and confident room of what's what, and embarked on the adventurous challenges of bringing knowledge to Congleton.

That was a year ago. I now hate Aiden. I hate the way he drives around town with the exclusive purpose of leaping out to help wave motorists into tricky parking spots. I hate the way he insists once every ten weeks on eating mouldy bread to clear his system out. I hate the superhuman effort he puts into implementing his scheme to advance human knowledge through a network of Tuesday night pub quizzes. Above all, I hate the way, when confronted by an enormous Red

Leicester ploughman's at lunchtime, he starts his meal by saying 'Let battle commence!'

My bookshop is dying under Richard; the law and economics sections are overgrown and have gone and suffocated a fiction section that once heaved with succulent Rushdies. I am a crestfallen woman, and They can supply nothing to relieve me of my perturbance. I'm told by family and friends that I'm suffering a breakdown, and I've no doubt that will be the inevitable diagnosis of my condition. I know this because my doctor told me. And he mentioned that they say it's happening more and more to my type these days. And I recognized the look on his face as he said it.

But I have written this account, and slipped it into the last surviving Weldon in the one remaining shelf I have any influence over in the hope that you, dear browser, whoever you are, can know what lies at the heart of the world, and let others know too, and decide whether it's significant enough to do anything about.